THE
LEADERS
CAPABILITIES

DR. GREGORY L. CRUELL

ISBN: 978-1-4834-4453-6 (sc)
ISBN: 978-1-4834-4452-9 (e)

Lulu Publishing Services rev. date: 03/02/2016

ACKNOWLEDGEMENTS

I would like to thank all of the leaders and laborers, both past and present, with whom I have served, and who have lived the principles of this book in conduct and deed. Your influence has made a difference in my life and the development of the Ethnos Leadership process. I am grateful for the relationships that we share, because *"without relationship, there is no leadership."*

To my precious wife for life, and best friend, Deirdre, who has been as Barnabas was to Paul, my God-sent encourager: your love and support have made me a better leader. Thank you.

To my children, Nicole, Stephanie, and Genese, you have been created to make a difference in the world. Always remember that you are all Ethnos Leaders.

To the reader, it is our sincere desire at Ethnos Leadership that in these pages, you will discover additional tools and truth that will assist you in a lifetime leadership journey that will make a difference in the world.

"It's never too late. You have yet to discover what you are capable of."

Mahatma Gandi

CONTENTS

Session III

Session IV

Creating Transformational Leaders Who Transform Others

THE WHAT AND WHY OF ETHNOS LEADERSHIP

Leadership and mentorship are the opposite sides of the same coin. For leadership to be authentic there must be mentorship—you cannot have one without the other. Our philosophy concerning this concept is seen in what we call the Ethnos Equation:

Mentorship: Purposeful Relationships+ Accountability=Professional Responsibility

Mentorship Diagram

The Merriam-Webster dictionary defines a professional or professionalism as *"the conduct, aims, or qualities that characterize or mark a particular profession."* This definition implies that professionalism encompasses a number of different attributes, and, together, these attributes identify and define a professional.

Mentorship is the non-negotiable epicenter of Ethnos Leadership. Mentorship in Ethnos Leadership is the *professional responsibility* that is acquired and required for organizational health and well-being.

At every level in the organization, the leader and the led need a mentor for *accountability*. Purposeful relationships are valued, trusted and respected. Bonds or alliances of this manner opens the door to forthright accountability. Being accountable or answerable to a trusted friend, advisor or mentor provides both protection and correction through life and leadership in an environment that is safe because it is trusted and valued. Responsibility simply means cultivating one's ability to respond to the distinct circumstances and situations of one's personal and organizational leadership influence via the Ethnos Leadership process (*Discover, Develop, Disciple, Make A Difference*).

The leader's *professional responsibility* is learned and acquired through the evolution of intentional *mentorship* by virtue of *purposeful relationships*. Purposeful relationships are rooted in the principle attributed to Saint Francis of Assisi, *"seek first to understand rather than to be understood."* An understanding of the organization's goals and the people or team that make the organization go and grow is informed by this basic universal principle.

The word nations in the original Greek is *"ethnos."* Ethnos maybe defined as *"a group of people bound together by the same customs, conduct, language, behaviors or other distinguishing features."*

There are 3 modules in the Ethnos Leadership Process. *Character, capabilities and competencies.* Each module has 4 sessions. At the conclusion of each individual session participants will create a summary of principles discovered and has decided to develop. This aspect of the Ethnos Leadership process is the *Personal Leadership Perspective* (PLP).

During week 13, participants will combine their 12 Personal Leadership Perspective summaries to create a cumulative plan or writing of the *Personal Leaders Character Story* (PLCS) that initiates Phase V of the process entitled: *"Commitment to Investing in Personal and Organizational Transformation."*

The entire Ethnos Leadership Process is designed to be completed in 13 weeks. The emphasis is again, a platform of *self-evaluation and self-reflection.* The conclusion of the process is a commitment to a lifetime of *discovering, developing* and *discipling* (mentoring) of those that we lead that are bound together by the Ethnos Leadership process making a *difference* across *"nations"* (*ethnos*- people's lives).

This book contains the 4 sessions of the capabilities module, or the *"Pursuit of The Future."* Capabilities describe the quality or condition that grants the leader the drive and ability to learn and acquire new skills for a given task or assignment. Capabilities can also be defined as qualities or potential that can be developed.

It is by pursuing future capabilities that the Ethnos Leader continues to *discover, develop, disciple* (mentor) to make a *difference* in the lives of others that makes a difference in our world.

"In all situations, it is my response that decides whether a crisis is escalated or de-escalated, and a person is humanized or de-humanized. If we treat people as they are, we make them worse. If we treat people as they ought to be, we help them to become what they are capable of becoming."

Johann Wolfgang von Goethe

For more information about the Ethnos Leadership Process contact us at: <u>ethnosleadership@gmail.com</u>

THE ART OF COMMUNICATION: CAN YOU HEAR ME NOW?

Foundation

For the purposes of this topic, Dictionary.com defines art as, *"the quality, production, expression, or realm, according to aesthetic principles of what is beautiful appealing, or of more than ordinary significance."* A very basic definition of communication is the exchange of information between two parties or groups. Therefore, in this sense, the aim of this session is to review the exchange of information as an art form of the quality, production, and expression of what is beautiful and appealing concerning communication.

In addition, an art form can be defined as an undertaking or activity enhanced by a high level of skill or refinement. Whatever the form of art may be—whether it is dancing, painting, music or, in this case communication—it takes many years of patient practice to become proficient.

1

One of the most challenging aspects of any relationship or interaction with another person is that of communication. Most of us, if not all of us would agree that there have been many conversations that we have been a part of, and we believed that we were communicating. However, as the conversation continued, it became clear that we were not communicating at all.

On February 22, 2004, USA Today ran a story concerning Verizon Wireless cell phone service which featured the *"Test Man."*

We know him better as the *"Can you hear me now?"* guy. In the article Verizon says, "Test Man" is the personification of a crew of 50 Verizon employees who each drive 100,000 miles annually in specially outfitted vehicles to test the reliability of Verizon's cell phone network.

One particular ad features Test Man roaming the country through wheat fields, across snowy mountains, through airports, along highways, in a bowling alley asking the simple question, "Can you hear me now?"

The simple *"Can you hear me now?"* question, all too familiar to cell phone users, helped Verizon move network reliability up the ranks as a key purchase consideration for wireless users at a time when other companies were shouting about minutes and prices.

"No one was talking about it," Marvin Davis, vice-president of Verizon advertising says. "We tried to communicate our relentless drive to make wireless even better. If you can't place the call, it doesn't matter how many minutes you have." The nature of Verizon's Test Man and his question, *"Can you hear me now?"* represents an authentic challenge for leaders at every level. In essence what Verizon's advertisement suggests is are we communicating?

For most of us in the United States, as it relates to our interactions and conversations with one another, we think English, before we think communication.

We inherently believe that because we are speaking the same language as the person that we are in dialogue with that this is communication. As most of us, if not all of us have discovered, this is not always true. Communication is the exchange of thoughts, opinions, or information.

If there is not an accurate exchange of thoughts or information, if the message is unclear, we are really not communicating. There most certainly maybe an exchange of words or language, but this does not always mean that communication has occurred. If we cannot communicate and even more importantly, *communicate effectively*, unnecessary problems are sure to follow.

According to Adler and Towne, all that ever has been accomplished by humans and all that ever will be accomplished involves communication with others. Adler and Townes position is that communication originates as *"mental images"* within a person who desires to convey those images to another. Mental images can include ideas, thoughts, pictures, and emotions. The person who wants to communicate is called the *sender*. [1]

To transfer an image to another person, the sender first must transpose or translate the images into symbols that receivers can understand.

Symbols often are words but can be pictures, sounds, or sense information, such as touch or smell. Only through symbols can the mental images of a sender have meaning for others. The process of translating images into symbols is called *encoding*. Once a message has been encoded, the next level in the communication process is to *transmit* or communicate the message to a *receiver*. The transmission of the information occurs in many ways. It occurs in face-to-face verbal interaction, over the telephone, through printed materials, (letters, newspapers, email etc.), or through visual media such as television or photographs.[2]

Other transmission channels include touch, gestures, clothing, and physical distances between sender and receiver. When a message is received by another person, a *decoding* process occurs. Just as a sender must encode messages in preparation for transmission through communication channels, receivers must sense and interpret the symbols and then decode the information back into images, emotions, and thoughts that make sense to them.

---

[1] Pfeiffer, William J. The Pfeiffer Library, Volume 25, 2nd Edition, Jossey-Bass, 1998.

[2] IBID.

When messages are decoded exactly as the sender has intended, the images of the sender and the images of the receiver match, and effective communication occurs.[3]

There are countless communication theories that have been studied and implemented across human history and relationships.

The aim of this session is not to discuss which theory is better than another. However, for communication to be effective, there is a right/wrong way or ethical way to approach the process of information exchange. Our attention is now focused on reviewing a means of essential or ethical elements for effective communication.

---

[3] IBID.

Part I: Essential Elements of Ethical and Effective Communication

Josina M. Makau in *"The 21st Century Communication A Reference Handbook"* says that, *"ethics is the study of values, of what is more or less important, of the good, of behavioral guidelines and norms."*[4] He also states that, *"communication is the use of available resources to convey information, to move, to inspire, to persuade, to enlighten, to connect; which is an inherently ethical undertaking."* [5]

Utilizing the preceding definition and perspective, communication involves *three key elements*:

1. Choice
2. Reflects values
3. Consequences

These three key elements are what shapes and forms the basis of communications ethical makeup. If this is true, ethical (right or wrong) communication requires understanding of and responsiveness to each of these three key elements. It is through this process that the ends, means and consequences of

---

[4] https://edge.sagepub.com/system/files/77593_1.1ref. pdf. Ethical and Unethical Communication. 21 Century Communication A Reference Handbook. Publisher: SAGE Publications, Inc., 2009, pg.1. Accessed October 15, 2015.
[5] IBID, Accessed October 15, 2015.

right or wrong communication produce intended or unintended results.

Choice

When we talk about choice, a basic definition carries the idea of the opportunity or right to choose between different things or courses of action. With the basic definition of communication being the exchange of information, what is suggested by this element is that there is a moral (choice) responsibility with in this exchange of information if it is to be ethical. Choice means that there is an alternative or another way. In other words, we have the power of choice in literally every facet of life and with this choice, specifically concerning communication, is the choice right or wrong?

For those that are involved in the exchange of information and this element of choice, it includes questions such as, will those involved *choose* to be open or closed minded about the exchange of information? Will those involved in the exchange *choose* to listen defensively? Will they *choose* to seek understanding from each other? When we encounter strangers, concerning the exchange of information, choice is still involved.

We have the *choice* to decide whether to recoil or to express hostility, on the one hand or to smile or otherwise express a sense of human connection on the other. Within this element of choice there are structural and relational factors that are relevant. This speaks to a person's particular position or power. Someone that is lower in the hierarchy of a particular organizational setting has a choice based on how they perceive the structure of the organization. Communication is always challenging without a context of openness and honesty. Without an open and honest context or environment, employees or followers will have questions such as, *"am I free to speak my mind in this organization?" "Am I free to express views and opinions that are contrary to company or organizational values?"*[6]

If communication is to be effective and ethical, the human connection element must *always* be considered. What this further means is a relational, open and honest exchange of information and it is always the moral, ethical communicator that displays these traits.

Reflects Values

In this interpersonal communication setting, each individual's approach is shaped by their particular set of goals, values, emotions, and perceptions.

In this interpersonal communication exchange questions such as, *"how does each person involved perceive the other?" "How thoroughly has each considered the consequences of this particular communication to self, to others, and to the working relationship?"* A person's particular response to questions such as the preceding

---

[6] IBID, 436.

are significantly influence by the values that each person possesses.[7] Every successful organization has in its foundation certain values and standards. It is these values and standards that define the culture of the organization, setting the tone for every interaction. When these values and standards are lacking, the likelihood of ethical breaches are more likely to occur. The ethically effective communicator helps to set the expectations for what type of behavior and conduct is acceptable and what is not acceptable by consistent exchange and modeling of the values and standards that have forged the organizations success.

The clearer the leader is on this point, the better people understand whether their personal actions and interactions with one another are consistent with the values that have been established within the organization. Where values do not exist or not clearly communicated, a vacuum is created in which doubt, cynicism, and distrust can rapidly take root in the organization.

When team members don't understand the standards and values of their leader, or the organization the relationship is limited and therefore effective, ethical communication is disrupted.

---

[7] IBID, 436.

Consequences

A consequence is the effect, result, or outcome of something that occurred earlier. James Faust stated, *"In this life, we have to make many choices. Some are very important choices. Some are not. Many of our choices are between good and evil. The choices we make, however, determine to a large extent our happiness or our unhappiness, because we have to live with the consequences of our choices."*

Choices inevitably lead us to consequences, both good and bad. Former First Lady Eleanor Roosevelt once stated, *"I am today a result of the choices that I made yesterday."* Right or wrong, good or bad, the choices that I make today will produce some form of consequences. An hour has 60 minutes and a day has 24 hours, 24x60 equals 1,440 minutes per day.

Most likely at some point, we have heard someone say or maybe even ourselves have said, *"It has been a bad day!"* Most likely at some point of that day, we have experienced, the results or effects of something that has occurred earlier that has not been so good.

The ethical, effective communicator develops the capacity (by choice) in the exchange of information to stay in the *"positive lane"* as much as possible and consequently help to reduce the frequency of those *bad days*. As ethically effective communicators we have a responsibility to anticipate likely consequences and to be prepared to respond to such consequences (good or bad) in a manner that upholds the values of what is right and wrong in how and what we communicate for effectiveness.

In their book *Leadership: Enhancing the Lessons of Experience* authors Richard Hughes, Robert Ginnett, and Gordon J Curphy, provide us with their definition of effective communication. Their posture is that effective communication involves the ability to transmit and receive information with a high probability that the intended message is passed from sender to receiver via what they call, *"a systems view of communication."*[8] According to the authors this model of communication is best understood as a process beginning with an intention to exchange certain information with others.

The authors define or describe their model with four aspects of a systems view of communication:

- Intention
- Expression
- Reception
- Interpretation

Intention

Intention is *"an act or thought of a desired result of action."* Within this first aspect of the system are

---

[8] Richard L. Hughes, Robert C. Ginnett and Gordon J. Curphy. Leadership: Enhancing The Lessons of Experience 3rd Edition. (San Francisco: Irwin McGraw-Hill Publisher) 1999, p.492.

questions such as, what do you want to accomplish? Is your purpose clear? Who needs to hear you?

Expression

The ethical, effective communicator considers how do I articulate in words my intention? Simply because we are using words as we talk does not always mean that we are communicating effectively. This element should include questions such as, what medium or means should be used? Is the information expressed with the receiver's frame of reference in mind? Is the information expressed in terms the receiver will understand? Is it too much information expressed to quickly? Have the important points been emphasized?

Reception

Reception carries the idea or manner in which something is received. In this component the ethical, effective communicator prepares for a successful exchange of information by ensuring that there are no competing messages or other *"noise"* variables present that could possibly hinder reception.

Reception also includes ensuring that the message or information is factual and accurate prior to its delivery.

Interpretation

Interpretation of the information can depend upon the method of delivery and the *"tone"* in which it was delivered. Although the meal that I ordered at a 5 star restaurant maybe very expensive, if the meal is delivered on a dirty plate, the reception of the meal, no matter how good the meal maybe reception will be tainted. The tone is the *attitude* in which the meal is delivered. The waiter may insist that this is a 5-star restaurant and be totally oblivious to the fact that my plate is dirty! The ethical, effective communicator practices both *delivery and tone* (right attitude) to guard against poor or improper interpretation in the exchange of information.[9]

A system is simply a combination of elements or things that form a plan, procedure or operation. From this perspective of a systems approach to communication, it contains elements of the exchange of information that have proven to be valuable in the process that also includes *active listening,* and developing the ability to *remain objective and to not become defensive.*

Active Listening

Looking for the meaning behind someone else's words is the essence of active listening. In other words, the ethically effective communicator needs

---

[9] IBID, p.493.

to keep an open mind open to the senders' ideas. This in turn implies not *interrupting the speaker and not planning what to say while the speaker is delivering the message.* From this perspective, this person is not listening for comprehension, they are just waiting for their opportunity to get their point out and on the table. In addition, active listeners withhold judgment about the sender's ideas until they have heard the entire message. This avoids the possibility of having one's mind made up and avoid jumping to conclusions about what the sender is going to say.

As an aid to this systems view of communication, statements such as:

> *From your point of view...*
> *It seems you...*
> *As you see it...*
> *You think...*
> *What I hear you saying is...*
> *Do you mean...?*
> *I'm not sure I understand*
> *what you mean; is it...?*
> *I get the impression...*
> *You appear to be feeling...*
> *Correct me if I'm wrong....*[10]

The preceding process provides a purposeful effort towards being an ethically, effective communicator. In addition to what has been previously stated, in the

---

[10] IBID, 499.

exchange of information process it is important to *train to remain objective and to not become defensive.*

Remain Objective and Do Not Become Defensive

To be objective is to not be influenced by personal feelings or pre-judgments. To be objective is to be open-minded. In the exchange of information, when someone feels threatened in a conversation or effort to communicate this is most likely the point and place where objectivity may be lost and creates an opportunity for defensive behavior to occur.

Defensiveness lessons a leaders or follower's ability to constructively make use of the information. Defensiveness may also cause a tendency to place blame on others or categorize some as being morally good or bad team members. Which can further lead to a questioning of one's motives in the organization. Defensiveness may also decrease follower's willingness to pass additional unpleasant information on to the leader or other followers. A useful warning sign that a leader or team member may be behaving defensively, or perhaps close mindedly, is if the exchange of information continues with, *"Yes, but...*[11]

As a conjunction, but carries the idea of *"on or to the contrary."* What this suggests is that although I've heard the information that you have stated, my thought or information is different or contrary to

---

[11] IBID, 500.

what the other person in the conversation has stated. This juncture of the exchange of information does not necessarily have to be negative. It could simply be a matter of perspective, or how different views are present in the exchange. What may be helpful in these types of situations is the principle of *"consideration in communication."*

Consideration In Communication

Consideration in communication is an uncommon level of respect that is unsurpassed by feelings, emotions or other internal, external stimuli. Developing the ability to respect another's point of view (even if you disagree) diffuses defensive attitudes. Consideration in communication has the end in mind; which is an effective exchange of information. This principle takes into account the other participants values, needs, and what is important from their particular viewpoint. To consider is to regard with respect. To consider also means to think carefully about a matter or to reflect upon.

Intention, expression, reception, interpretation, active listening, remaining objective without becoming defensive and consideration in communication is a viable systems approach to communication. There are certainly other models available for the ethically effective communicator and leader. Thoughtful practice of the preceding seven principles may help to avoid the ever present barriers that inevitably arise to effective communication.

PART II: BARRIERS TO EFFECTIVE COMMUNICATION

. . . .

The dictionary tells us that *"a barrier is anything that restrains progress, or boundaries of any kind."* Whenever or however barriers arise, it inevitability leads to the reality of something is missing in our communication or the question of *"what's missing in the exchange of information?"* When a component of communication is missing because of some sort of barrier, many times we unknowingly open the door to:

> *Mis*-communication: exchange of
>   information is incorrect or tainted
> *Mis*-perception: how another may see
>   the matter information
> *Mis*-interpretation: inaccurate meaning
>   of information
> *Mis*-understanding: how another
>   comprehends the information
> *Mis*-conception: of an idea or plan
>   to hold as an opinion; to believe
> *Mis*-take: error in action, opinion or
>   judgment concerning the information
> *Mis*-trust: lack of trust or confidence
> *Mis*-treat: to abuse or treat badly
> *Mis*-lead: to govern or guide wrongly
> *Mis*-represntation: incorrect
>   representation

The prefix *"mis"* simply means wrong. Barriers such as the preceding are as destructive and toxic as any poison that is purposely introduced into an organization.

These barriers have the potential to create *disunity* where the organizational aim is unity. When leaders or team members recognize the entrance of any of these barriers into the organizational environment, the door that may have unknowingly been opened must be closed to safeguard the health and well-being of the team.

Another barrier to effective communication is the possibility of acquiring what is known as *"occupational or industrial deafness."*[12] It is caused by prolonged exposure to noise which results in the damage of the nerve cells of the inner ear. The resulting hearing impairment will be permanent, leading to hearing loss.

Symptoms include:

- Difficulty in communicating with others in person or over phone
- Feeling the need to raise the volume of radio and television
- Difficulty in concentrating

Occupational deafness normally occurs in industries that have loud, noisy environments.

[12] https://www.osha.gov/SLTC/noisehearingconservation/. Accessed October 17, 2015.

Particularly in occupations such as shipbuilding, coal mining, metal manufacturing and factory environments where noisy machinery is used.[13]

However, it is also important to note that occupational deafness may also occur when the "loud noise" of negative, contrary practices and opinions of team members release the noise of their displeasure. When one person is not pleased in the organization, and they begin to express their dissatisfaction with others that are not satisfied, this dissatisfaction now has the potential to become very loud and internally damaging.

It is important or urgent that when negative, contrary practices and opinions or barriers are noticed, that leaders take the necessary steps to determine the cause of such contrary noise or opinions within the environment.

If a person of a leader's team is dissatisfied, what must be discovered is *why* is the team member dissatisfied?

Are their personal matters (i.e. health, home, etc.) that the team member is experiencing that contributes to the *"dissatisfaction or organizational noise level?"* Particularly if the person has produced well within the organization, but over a period of time, job performance has decreased. Discovering the root of the dissatisfaction will not only assist the organization,

---

[13] IBID.

but will also help the team member to get back on a positive track. This is the leader's responsibility.

Another important factor in barriers to effective communication is one's current emotional state (mental/health). As a soldier while serving in the Army, if I was sick or not feeling 100 percent, to some extent I trained myself to *not go* to the doctor.

My mindset was that I simply had too much to do and I did not have time to be sick. The mission was too important. However, I had trained myself incorrectly! Our mental health and physical health is vitally important to not only the mission of our organization but also to the people that serve with us. If we are not at our best both mentally and physically, at some point we will lose an edge in communicating effectively. As leaders and communicators if there are an abundance of projects, meetings, appointments, these all require time and concentrated effort for success in each arena.

Another way to make this point is that it is important that we learn how to manage our time and not allow our time to manage us or stress us. Learning to effectively manage our time increases our well-being which in turn, will increase our ability to communicate effectively. Self-leadership is the foundation of all leadership. We must first lead ourselves effectively in order to lead others effectively. Being able to answer honestly, "How am *I* doing?" keeps us mindful of the importance of being well in order to communicate effectively to and with those that we lead.

PART III: WHAT HAPPENS WHEN WE FAIL TO COMMUNICATE EFFECTIVELY

"Be sincere; be brief; be seated."

Franklin D Roosevelt

Our former president's admonishment is certainly a clear ally to minimizing the possibility of failed or ineffective communication. Communication is an area in leadership that is often discussed as being critical to any successful organization. Even though there are numerous discussion about its importance, in many instances effective communication still alludes us. So what is the real cost of failing to communicate effectively?

Loss of Time

One thing that most people seem to be short on these days, despite all of the advances in technology, is time. It was Benjamin Franklin that asked the question, *"Dost thou love life? Then do not squander time, for that's the stuff that life is made of."* We all have the same allocation per week, per day, per year. When leaders fail to effectively communicate, valuable time and energy is wasted because the task or assignment will have to be done again (properly) if it is to be of value! And as you are paying your employee's or team members for doing it over again, you are adversely impacting the bottom line financial results of the company or organization.

Loss of Audience

People have very different preferences and needs when it comes to communication. Understanding one's audience (team members) lends to the necessity of a variety of communication styles. Some people find it easy to understand information when it is presented in tables, Others prefer diagrams, and others still need narrative. Some want it in writing, some need to hear it. Some want to start at the conclusion, others want to be walked through your process. The more important the message the more we need to tune it to the variety of people in our audience or our team. Where there are multiple preferences, then we need to use multiple styles to ensure everyone gets some of what they need.

Loss Of Confidence

People want leaders to lead and provide clear direction to others. When leaders procrastinate or avoid making decisions, they create doubt and this doubt can lead to a loss of confidence among followers.

It creates ambiguity and uncertainty. This further leads to team members doing what *they believe* should be done (activity) without a degree of certainty. You can run in a race and cross the finish line ahead of everyone else in the pack and discover that it was the wrong race. Team members need to know which race to run for effectiveness because activity does not always equate to productivity.

Loss Of Credibility

People only follow people who they believe have credibility. How you communicate with others has a direct impact on your credibility. For example, if you do not treat people well your credibility will diminish. Credibility is rooted in trust and trust is a part of what we believe is trustworthy. If a leader loses credibility with team members or employee's, it will be nearly impossible to get their best efforts. When and where trust has eroded, bankruptcy of team effort is inevitable. Les Csorba says in his book, Trust, The One Thing That Makes or Breaks A Leader, *"fundamentally, leadership is built on trust. Trust is slow to form, but can come apart very quickly."*[14]

Whatever our status or position in life may be, whether celebrity, politician, athlete, or a stay home mom or dad, if there is no trust in the information, there is no effective communication. If effective communication is one of a leader's greatest assets, then poor communication will certainly be one of,

---

[14] Csorba, p.xxiv.

if not the greatest liability. The key to developing any skill is practice. There are those that believe that simply because we speak the same language that communication is occurring. George Bernard Shaw once said that, *"the single biggest problem in communication is the illusion that it has taken place."*

To minimize or to reduce the likelihood of poor or ineffective communication, purposeful practice to ensure effective communication is a must. Some ways to practice effective communication may include:

1. *Before* the exchange of information attempt to identify any potential differences in definitions, or team member experiences, etc., which might lead to difficulties later.
2. Allow room for dialogue and listen carefully and completely to what team members are saying.
3. Be willing to ask questions for clarity as needed.
4. Frequent communication with the team reduces anxiety and uncertainty.
5. Stay in the present moment physically and emotionally. Avoid distractions or noise that can distract you or your team from the exchange of information.
6. Pay attention to what is being expressed. Acknowledge what you are feeling and the other person in the exchange. Note the tone of

voice, facial expression of others involved in the exchange.

7. Seeing others as mirrors. Can you relate to your team member's experiences? A common experience creates additional footing for understanding and trust.

Communication is a systems process in which participants not only exchange information news, and ideas but also create and share meaning. In general, communication is a means of connecting people or places. What happens when we fail to communicate effectively, disrupts the process and disconnects people. Trust begins to evaporates, confusion and misunderstanding appear and organizational loyalty begins to wane. Developing the capacity and capability of being an effective communicator is not an option for today's leader. Consideration in communication, means to regard with respect. To respect the process of developing the capability of effective communication is to further respect and regard the people that we communicate with.

In so doing, a mutual respect and regard will be created and sustained throughout the organization to which we belong.

Summation–The Art of Communication: Can You Hear Me Now?

As we began this session, the Test Man from Verizon Wireless asked us the question "can you hear me now?" Test Man" is the personification of a crew of 50 Verizon employees who each drive 100,000 miles annually in specially outfitted vehicles to test the reliability of Verizon's cell phone network. The nature of Verizon's Test Man and his question, "Can you hear me now?" represents an authentic challenge for leaders at every level. In essence what Verizon's advertisement suggests is are we communicating and more importantly, are we communicating effectively?

Accepting the very basic definition of communication as the exchange of information, every leader in this exchange is exerting their influence upon their particular audiences or team members. As stated in the foundation of this session, communication was likened to an art form. An art form is defined as *"an undertaking or activity enhanced by a high level of skill or refinement."*

In the fast pace world in which we live today developing the skill as an effective communicator is an art form. Communication is about more than just exchanging information.

Effective communication is how you convey a message so that it is received and understood by someone in exactly the way you intended. Effective communication is the art of combining *"essential elements of ethical and effective communication."* Effective communication is recognizing and acting to open *"doors or barriers to effective communication."*

An understanding of *"what happens when we fail to communicate effectively"* alerts every authentic leader to not fall asleep at the wheel. This is a matter of responsibility and accountability for the leader to the organization to know and safeguard their team from potentially destructive elements or negative influences.

Effective communication helps the leader to deepen connections to others and improve teamwork, decision-making, and problem solving. Effective, ethical communication assists in developing the capacity to recognize and understand one's own emotions and those to whom you're communicating with. It enables you to communicate even negative or difficult messages without creating conflict or destroying trust.

Dedicated, devoted time and effort is necessary to develop these skills and become an effective ethical, communicator. The more effort and practice invested to this end, the greater *"artist"* of effective, ethical communication the leader becomes.

QUESTIONS FOR REFLECTION

1. What elements from the session would you use to create active listening skills among those that you lead?

2. A systems view of communication includes intention, expression, reception and interpretation. What steps can you employ to ensure that the reception and interpretation of your communication as a leader is understood and accurate?

3. Concerning Josina Makau's three key elements of effective communication, *"choice, reflection of values and consequences,"* how would you adapt these elements to fit your organization?

4. What could be done to minimize barriers to effective communication in your work environment or organization?

5. As a leader, it has become apparent to you that effective communication in your organization is not a priority. How would you persuade or convince your superiors or supervisors of the need to improve organizational communication?

QUOTES OF PRINCIPLED LEADERS

"Communication to a relationship is like oxygen to life. Without it, it dies."

Tony Gaskins

"Without communication, there is no relationship. Without respect, there is no trust and without trust there is no reason to continue."

Unknown

"Speak (communicate) in such a way that others love to listen to you. Listen in such a way that others love to speak to you."

Anonymous

"Most people do not listen with the intent to understand. Most people listen with the intent to reply."

Stephen R. Covey

"If you cannot communicate and get your ideas across you are giving up your potential. Learn how to communicate well."

Warren Buffett

"Never mistake knowledge for wisdom. One helps you make a living; the other helps you make a life."

Eleanor Roosevelt

CONFLICT: HANDLE IT OR IT WILL HANDLE YOU

Foundation

"Seek first to understand, then to be understood."

Saint Francis of Assisi

According to the Natural Resource Management and Environment Department of the United Nations (NRMED), conflict is a *"clash of interests, values, actions, views or directions."* The underlying cause of conflict is disagreement among people. People disagree because they see things differently, want different things, have thinking styles which encourage them to disagree, or are predisposed to disagree.[15]

In her book, *"The Highly Effective Executive, How To Reduce Conflict, Inspire Action and Make A Difference In*

---

[15] http://www.fao.org/docrep/W7504E/w7504e07.htm. Accessed May 9, 2015.

Your Organization," Anutza Bellissimo says that the five most common causes of organizational conflict are:

1. Difference in methods and priorities
2. Competition for supremacy
3. Misunderstandings
4. Differences over perceptions of values
5. Stubbornness and sensitivity [16]

Bellissimo's five most common causes of organizational conflict in essence says that in productive organizations conflict is going to occur. Considering these five most common causes, the capable leader handles conflict by creating and maintaining a strategy for resolving conflict when it arises that begins with understanding.

If conflict is indeed a *"clash of interests, values, actions, views or directions,* the capable, conflict skilled leader recognizes the need to be prepared to turn that which could be perceived as negative into that which is positive.

According to SmallBusiness.com, there are two main types of conflict, *"healthy and unhealthy,"* and they both have several identifiable characteristics. Healthy conflict builds the team by causing those involved to review their attitudes and those of the organization

---

[16] Bellissimo, Anutza. The Highly Effective Executive: How To Reduce Conflict, Inspire Action and Make a Difference In your Organization. (Scottsdale: Bellissimo Publishing, 2015, P.3.

and to honestly ask the question, *"What is going on?"* The answer to the question will only come by way of an effective problem resolution process due to increased involvement of all affected team members. This contrasts with unhealthy conflict where team morale and unity is destroyed and team members become divided and polarized. Unhealthy conflict leaves the problem unresolved, and drains resources and energy from team members, the organization and the core project at hand.[17]

All of us, at some time or another have been involved in some type of conflict. Depending upon the severity, or how the conflict was handled, it was an easy or not so easy experience because of one's preparedness for the conflict. There is no *"one-size-fits-all"* for handling conflict. The aim of this session, as in previous sessions, is to continue to *discover,* and *develop* the skill to be able to handle conflict, which is essential for an Ethnos Leader. If as a leader the conflict is not handled, it will handle the leader. Conflict cannot be avoided and this session is intended to provide insight to a process and pattern by which conflict can be understood and resolved.

---

[17] http://smallbusiness.chron.com/healthy-unhealthy-conflict-2832.html. Accessed May 9, 2015.

PART I: CONFLICT IS INEVITABLE

Leadership and conflict go hand-in-hand simply because people are involved with varying viewpoints. If you cannot or will not address conflict in a healthy, productive fashion, you should not be in a leadership role. Resolving conflict is like any other leadership task or assignment; it is an acquired skill. As much as a leader or team member may try to avoid conflict, you can never escape conflict of some sort because of diverse ideas and perspectives.

Daniel Dana in his book "Conflict Resolution," defines conflict as *"a condition between or among team members whose jobs are interdependent, who are frustrated or angry, who perceive others as being at fault, and who act in ways that cause a problem within the organization."*[18]

1. Interdependent
2. Emotional
3. Blame others
4. Behavior has caused a problem

Interdependent

In any size organization, where a team effort is required, interdependency is a normal pattern to

---

[18] Daniel Dana. Conflict Resolution. (New York: McGraw-Hill Publishers), 2013, p.5.

complete a task or assignment. Everyone needs something from someone else to complete the assignment. There is a certain amount of vulnerability that comes along with this component that is not always comfortable. When cooperation amongst team members does not occur smoothly, conflict is inevitable.

Blame Others

At this point, those that are involved in the conflict may blame each other for causing the problem. As an example, someone may criticize the other for being inconsiderate or selfish and now the issue has become *personal* and no longer solely organizational and conflict is inevitable.

Emotional

Once someone blames another inevitably emotions become involved. Sometimes even to the point of anger but many times that anger is hidden that can lead to passive-aggressive behavior. This type of conduct involves a range of behaviors designed to get back at another person without recognizing the underlying anger. This may appear in the form of politeness and cordiality, but underneath the outward appearance, other coworkers might not be able to see the true emotions concerning this matter.

Behavior Has Caused A Problem

When certain behavior has caused a problem, productivity and job performance is affected by a lack of cooperation with one another. It is certainly *ultra*-personal at this point and it becomes clear that those that are involved have developed a dislike for each other. However, this is not necessarily the organizations problem. When personal conflicts begin to affect job performance, this is the time and place for intervention.

The four factors briefly highlighted above include *feelings* or (emotions), *perceptions* or (thoughts), and *actions* or (behaviors). Psychologists consider *"emotions, thoughts and behaviors"* to be the three dimensions of human experience. The human experience is the knowledge that we have gained in these categories that have assisted in the shaping and molding of self. In each of these dimensions we will find conflict because it is rooted in all three aspects of human nature. [19]

Conflict concealed, avoided or otherwise ignored, will likely fester only to grow into resentment, create withdrawal or cause factional infighting within an organization; this is all a part of the human nature experience. If this is all a part of the human nature

---

[19] www.sagepub.com/hutchisonpe4e/.../88797_04cs.doc. Accessed May 18, 2015.

experience, what creates conflict in the workplace? Consider the following:

1. Power struggles
2. Egotism
3. Pride
4. Jealousy
5. Conceit
6. Performance discrepancies
7. Compensation issues
8. No or little concern for others
9. Someone simply having a bad day

With the previous suggestions as to what creates conflict in the workplace would appear to lead to the conclusion that just about anything and everything has the potential to create conflict. The reality is that the root of most conflict is either born out of *poor communication* or the *inability to control one's emotions*. All conflict arises from these two major causes of conflict.[20]

Communication: Where there is poor information, no information, or misinformation, conflict will arise. Clear, concise, accurate, and timely communication of information provides a safeguard against conflict and will help to lessen both the number and the severity of conflicts.

---

[20] http://www.forbes.com/sites/mikemyatt/2012/02/22/5-keys-to-dealing-with-workplace-conflict/. Accessed October 18, 2015.

Emotions: There will always be those that are determined to have things their way, even if it is the wrong way to achieve the organizations mission. Our emotions are indicators of what we are feeling. To make decisions simply based on what or how we may feel at the moment can prove to be disastrous for the future.

For the capable leader, understanding the reality that conflict is *inevitable* carries the responsibility of preparation for the *inevitable*.

If poor communication and the inability to control one's emotions as the breeding ground for most conflict, a continual development of *temperance or self-control* may be the solution. Of vital importance to self-control is that, before leaders can expect to lead anyone else successfully, they must first lead and control their own *"self."* In so doing, the self-controlled or temperate leader sets an example worth emulating. Cultivating the virtue and ability of temperance (self-control) does not deny what a person is feeling, it is simply not allowing our feelings to dictate how we communicate.

PART II: CONFLICT IS MANAGEABLE AND RESOLVABLE

••

In this section we want to look at different viewpoints concerning *how* conflict is both manageable and resolvable. To some extent conflict is normally viewed as negative. However, there can be some positive effects of conflict as well. Such as an impetus for change, better decision-making, key issues are surfaced, and people's feelings get aired. [21] Seeking resolution to conflicts is not always easy but any successful organization cannot avoid conflict. Whether it's negative or positive.

Creating or developing a pragmatic approach to resolving conflict should be in the tool bag of every organization minded capable leader.

A key in this approach to conflict management and resolution is to invest the time to understand and clarify the conflict, to be able to separate personal feelings from the problem and to focus on the collective interests of the organization. A very effective approach of managing and resolving conflict is a model of *negotiation*. This model is centered on

---

[21] Hughes, Rich, Ginnett, Robert, and Curphy Gordy. Leadership Enhancing The Lessons of Experience, 3rd Edition. (New York: Irwin McGraw-Hill), 1999, p.547.

and seeking *win-win outcomes* for all that are involved. The model of negotiation has three elements:

1. Prepare for The Negotiation
2. Separate The People From The Problem
3. Focus On Interests, Not Positions [22]

Prepare for The Negotiation

Benjamin Franklin once stated that, *"by failing to prepare, you are preparing to fail."* A considerable amount of time may be required to prepare for the session. As a capable leader, skilled in conflict resolution, anticipating each side's key concerns and issues, attitudes, goals and outcomes greatly enhances the process of negotiating or navigating through the conflict smoothly and positively

Separate The People From The Problem

There are several things that the capable leader can do to separate the people from the problem. First, leaders should not let their fears taint their perception of each side's intentions. What this also means is that leaders must get over the fear of conflict.

The people are not the problem; the problem is the problem! *Maintain the focus* of the negotiation on the problem and not personal feelings or agendas.

---

[22] IBID, p.549.

It is easy to assign or prescribe negative qualities to others when one feels threatened or fearful. When this occurs the ability to be objective in solving the conflict is hindered. Communicating clearly and succinctly, maintaining the focus on resolving the conflict without personal agendas provides the clearest path to resolution.

Focus On Interests, Not Positions

This element depends on understanding the difference between *interests and positions*. When Mr. B come's to the negotiation, his position may not be in the best interest of the organization simply because he believes that his position is right. Mr. B insists that his position is the better way. However, as a capable leader *I have prepared* for the negotiation, and *have separated the people from the problem*, I suggest an alternative to the position or demand that Mr. B presented that is a win-win and in the best interests of the organization and provides Mr. B satisfaction as a team member that his position is valid, valuable and a contributing factor to resolving the conflict.

Another practical model of conflict resolution is a problem-solving model that has five components:

1. Identify Problems or Opportunities For Improvement
2. Analyzing the Causes
3. Developing Alternative Solutions

4. Selecting and Implementing the Best Solution
5. Assessing The Impact of The Solution [23]

Identify Problems or Opportunities For Improvement

To identify something is to be able to establish what a particular matter or thing is. This step involves stating the problem so that everyone involved in developing solutions has an informed understanding in order to accurately diagnose and handle the problem. It will take time and most likely group discussion. Do not assume that everyone or anyone knows what the problem is. Someone once said that, *"the largest room in the world is the room for improvement."* This aspect does not have to be negative; it can be positive. Identifying personal shortfalls or organizational shortcomings helps to make the leader and the team better! Therefore, it is critical to invest the proper time for understanding the best solution for improvement of the organization by identifying the problem accurately.

Analyzing the Causes

Once the conflict or problem is identified the next step is to determine *how or why* it happened. Fact gathering, information sharing amongst all that are involved assist in the process of an accurate analysis.

[23] IBID, p.552.

Consider every aspect that team members bring to the table.

Everyone is different, and everyone may have a different perspective to add in analyzing the cause. Without a solid, well thought out analysis, important information may be missed that leads to misinformation that has the potential to deepen or add more fuel to the conflict.

Developing Alternative Solutions

This phase is what has been simply called in times past *brainstorming*. Everyone involved is actively engaged in the process of determining solutions to the problem or to the conflict. It is the generation of ideas and concepts that will be considered by all as possible solutions. This aspect requires a level of maturity amongst those that are a part of this process. It is not a *competition* as to whose idea is better. It is rather a *cooperation* of a solid team that is concerned about resolving a matter that has affected everyone.

Selecting and Implementing the Best Solution

After developing alternative solutions and a determination of the best solution, it is important to note that the first solution selected is not always the best solution, even if everyone involved finds it acceptable.

Questions that may be asked include:

- Have we examined the cause enough to ensure we have all pertinent information to determine what the best solution is?
- Do we have all the information needed to make a good decision among the alternatives suggested?
- Have we discovered as many alternatives as possible?
- What impact will the selected solution have on the entire organization?
- How do we as an organization implement the solution that we have selected?

Assessing The Impact of The Solution

The selected solution's continuing impact upon the organization must be assessed at some point in time. This involves asking the question, *"Did we get it right?"* If we did not get it right we have to go back and make it right! The integrity and productivity of the organization is dependent upon the leadership to lead in resolving conflict.[24]

Two models of conflict resolution have been presented for consideration. These are certainly not the only models of conflict resolution available. However, the principles of each model provides a clear direction

---

[24] IBID, 557.

for developing the ability for solving conflict. In this next section, as another means of handling conflict we will examine the theory and practice of Emotional Intelligence or EQ.

PART III: EMOTIONAL INTELLIGENCE AND CONFLICT

··

"10% of conflict is due to difference in opinion and 90% is due to delivery and tone."

Anonymous

According to SmallBusiness.com, there are two main types of conflict, *"healthy and unhealthy,"* and they both have several identifiable characteristics. Healthy conflict has the ability to build and unite the organizational team while unhealthy conflict has the potential to destroy and separate the team. To say that something is healthy, it also carries the connotation of *beneficial, conducive, profitable* and even *desirable*. From this perspective, healthy conflict has the potential of uniting an otherwise separated or divided team of co-workers. There are those that may be content with completing their work responsibilities in isolation. However, isolation of team members does little for the cultivation of organizational teamwork.

Healthy conflict, if managed well can produce a greater sense of oneness because it brings *everyone* involved in the conflict together and the conflict becomes a stimulus for dialogue, growth and maturity amongst the team that potentially increases productivity. Unhealthy conflict carries the idea of being *ill, feeble, diseased and in decline*. Organizations that are burdened and weighed down with these type of characteristics will not survive. No one will want to work or be a part of an organization where these type of problems are evident.

Peter Salovey and John D. Mayer are credited with the term 'Emotional Intelligence' (EQ) describing it in 1990 as *"a form of social intelligence that involves the ability to monitor one's own and others' feelings and emotions, to distinctly identity these feelings and emotions, and to use this information to guide one's thinking and action."*[25] Further defined, EQ is the ability to identify, use, understand, and manage emotions in positive ways to relieve stress, communicate effectively, empathize with others, overcome challenges, and defuse conflict.

If you have high emotional intelligence you are able to recognize your own emotional state and the emotional states of others, and engage with people in a way that draws them to you. It is by this understanding of emotions that leaders are better able to relate to their team members, form healthier relationships, and increase organizational productivity.[26] In their book *"Emotional Intelligence: Achieving Academic and Career Excellence,"* Darwin Nelson and Gary Low state that, *"emotional intelligence consists of specific skills, behaviors and attitudes that can be learned, applied and modeled by*

---

[25] http://www.emotionalintelligencecourse.com/eq-history. Accessed October 23, 2015.

[26] http://www.helpguide.org/articles/emotional-health/ emotional-intelligence-eq.htm. Accessed May 11, 2015.

leaders at every level."[27] Further, emotional intelligence is an amalgamation of developed skills and abilities to accurately *"know yourself, and behave responsibly as a person of worth and dignity."*

It is a continuing process of developing specific emotional skills. Personal awareness, understanding, and meaning of one's emotional self are at the heart of developing EQ.[28] Concerning conflict the model of EQ is of importance because of the pattern that it displays for *control of our emotional self.* Which many times is a leading factor in conflict arising in any organization. EQ involves certain emotional capabilities, but also eight distinct social principles or precepts:

- Self-awareness
- Self-esteem
- Self-regulation/control
- Empathy
- Assertiveness
- Persuasion
- Leadership
- Cooperation[29]

---

[27] Nelson, Darwin B. and Low, Gary R. Emotional Intelligence: Achieving Academic and Career Excellence. (Upper Saddle River: Prentice Hall Press), 2003, p. xiii.
[28] IBID, p.23.
[29] Ian Tuhovsky. Emotional Intelligence. A Practical Guide To Making Friends With Your Emotions and Raising Your EQ. Printed By Create Space, February 2015, p.22.

Self-Awareness

Self-awareness is the ability to identify and understand your own emotions, habits, and tendencies. Self-awareness enables a leader to understand not only other people, but also one's own attitude and response patterns at any given moment across a variety of situations or circumstances.

It is the development of a clear appreciation for why we do what we do that makes us distinct and unique.[30] In the moment of conflict, being aware of self provides a more honest and productive platform for resolving the problem. It is not denying self, it is being aware of self.

Self-Esteem

This is the ability to view oneself as positive, competent, and successful. In psychology, the term self-esteem is used to describe a person's overall sense of self-worth or personal value. Self-esteem is often seen as a personality trait, which means that it tends to be stable and enduring. Self-esteem can involve a variety of beliefs about the self, such as the appraisal of one's own appearance, beliefs, emotions, and behaviors.[31]

---

[30] IBID, p. 22.
[31] http://www.psychology.about.com. Cherry, Kendra. *"What Is Self Esteem?"* Accessed October 22, 2015.

Self-Regulation (Control)

Education.com says that *"self-regulation is the ability to monitor and control our own behavior, emotions, or thoughts, altering them in accordance with the demands of the situation."*

It includes the abilities to inhibit first responses, to resist interference from irrelevant distractions or external "noise," and to stay on relevant tasks even when not enjoyed.[32] Self-regulation is the developed ability to engage in mindful, intentional, and thoughtful behaviors. Self-regulation is the developed capability to control self, emotionally and psychologically in order to conduct one's self in the appropriate manner.

Empathy

Is a vital link between self and others in EQ. It is caring enough about others to feel and experience what others feel though the use of our imagination as if we were feeling it ourselves. To be empathetic is to respond and do something about what others may need.[33] Sympathy means to have compassion or sorrow for another but does not necessarily mean to feel what others feel. Zach Brittle of the Gottman

[32] http://www.education.com/reference/article/self-regulation-development-skill/. Accessed October 22, 2015.
[33] http://greatergood.berkeley.edu/topic/empathy/definition. Accessed October 22, 2015.

Institute stated that *"empathy and understanding must precede advice."*[34] As the skill of empathy is developed in moments of conflict, the possibility of resolution increases exponentially simply because of considering and imagining how the other person feels about the matter.

Assertiveness

This is the ability to clearly and honestly communicate personal thoughts and feelings to another person in a direct, appropriate and straightforward manner. It is a declaration of your beliefs while maintaining respect for others. Without developing assertiveness one may become interpersonally passive which weakens a leader's ability to accomplish tasks or assignments. In this area of assertiveness with other people, there are two potential problem areas that Nelson and Low state that capable leaders need to be aware of and avoid; and that is *aggression and deference.*[35]

Aggression

This is a personal communication style or pattern that violates, overpowers, dominates, or discredits another person. Defined it is the practice or habit of

---

[34] https://www.pinterest.com/pin/252764597812002398/. Accessed October 22, 2015.
[35] Nelson and Low, p.25.

launching attacks that includes hostile, destructive behavior or actions. It involves the emotion of anger that must be understood and converted. Anger includes annoyance, displeasure and irritation. When anger enters the picture, it has the potential to hinder and harm relationships. Anger and conflict achieves nothing. It is important to note that the difference between assertion and aggression is that assertion is *respectful* concerning others and aggression is *disrespectful*.[36]

Deference

Deference is a courteous regard for people's feelings. Deference can also mean yielding to another's judgment, opinion or will. Yielding to another's position or perspective can result in ineffective communications that negatively affect relationships. [37]

Persuasion

Businessdictionary.com defines persuasion as *"a process aimed at changing a person's or a group's attitude or behavior toward some event, or idea."*

Persuasion is further defined as the capability to impact and impress upon others the need to operate consistently in a positive manner that makes

---

[36] IBID,p.25.
[37] IBID, p. 24-25.

a positive difference organizationally. This is the place where momentum, direction, and guidance provide a sense of purpose for accomplishing goals of the organization. Positive, persuasive influence establishes a sense of *"I want to"* follow and creates team members and employees that believe in a leader that exemplifies and practices this trait of positive persuasive influence.

Leadership

The EQ capable leader takes on the obligation and duty to get the mission or task done due to the virtue of his or her ethics. Leadership is a dedication and devotion to the fulfillment of inspiring others to. The EQ capable leader takes absolute responsibility for the *"cause"* of inspiring others to mission or task completion because it must be done and there is no other option. Sheryl Sandberg, Chief Operating Officer of Facebook once stated that, *"leadership is about making others better as a result of your presence and making sure that impact lasts in your absence."* Communicated another way, someone once stated that *"character is what you do in the dark."* To this very honorable precept I would add that *"leadership is what **others do** in the dark"* as well, or simply the influence and impact senior leadership has made on team when they are *not* present. What this means is that the team handles the conflict or problem because they have been empowered, equipped and enabled by their senior leadership to do so.

Cooperation

Cooperation is the process of working together to the same end. It is the ability to understand, respond and work with others both personally and organizationally. This is a part of "*team*" work, and this is a part of "*me*" work. Whatever the circumstances or situations, we are a community of unity and we are better together.

In addition, cooperation is a reminder that for the health of the organization change and growth are necessary. If there is growth, there will be change. If there is change, there is a need to cooperate with change. The silkworm had to first crawl through the dirt and the mud (which was not pleasant) prior to being incubated in its cocoon, only to come forth as a butterfly. The process of cooperating with others, even when it maybe unpleasant, is necessary to reach the end-state which is fulfillment of the organizations mission. Having a mindset of cooperation at the table of disagreement or conflict reminds the EQ leader to be not a part of the *problem*, but rather a part of the *solution.*

Conflict can be positive and it most certainly can be negative. In stressful situations instead of a response, many react, which brings us back to the element of social awareness. If you cannot lead self, if you cannot manage self, you cannot lead anyone else. EQ consists of specific skills, behaviors and attitudes that can be learned, applied and modeled by leaders at every level anytime and anywhere.

Further, EQ is a consolidation of developed skills and abilities to accurately know yourself, and behave responsibly as a person of worth and dignity which is all connected to choice. When conflict arises (and it will) the EQ leader makes the choice to intervene with the appropriate response for resolving the matter. As a leader that is a part of the job description.

Although conflict occurs, development in the practice of EQ prepares the capable leader to be a tool in any organization as to how to handle conflict in order that conflict does not handle the organization.

SUMMATION: CONFLICT HANDLE IT OR IT WILL HANDLE YOU

According to the Natural Resource Management and Environment Department of the United Nations (NRMED), conflict is a *"clash of interests, values, actions, views or directions."* The underlying cause of conflict is disagreement among people.

People disagree because they see things differently, want different things, have thinking styles which encourage them to disagree, or are predisposed to disagree. Anutza Bellissimo says that the five most common causes of organizational conflict are:

1. Difference in methods and priorities
2. Competition for supremacy
3. Misunderstandings
4. Differences over perceptions of values
5. Stubbornness and sensitivity

The ability to recognize conflict, understand the nature of conflict, and to be able to bring swift and just resolution to conflict will always serve the capable leader well. According to SmallBusiness.com, there are two main types of conflict, *"healthy and unhealthy,"* and they both have several identifiable characteristics.

Healthy conflict has the ability to build and unite the organizational team while unhealthy conflict has the potential to destroy and separate the team. Conflict is either born out of poor communication or the inability to control one's emotions. Conflict is inevitable, manageable and resolvable and capable leader must have a course of action for resolution prepared. The key to conflict resolution is to invest the time to understand and clarify the conflict, to be able to separate personal feelings from the problem and to focus on the collective interests of the organization.

To accomplish the preceding action, it is essential that the capable leader has a particular model to apply to conflict when it arises. As another means of resolving conflict, emotional intelligence grants the developing leader the ability to identify, use, understand, and manage emotions in positive ways to relieve stress, communicate effectively, and empathize with peers, superiors and those that they lead to overcome challenges, and defuse conflict.

Darwin Nelson and Gary Low have stated that *"emotional intelligence consists of specific skills, behaviors and attitudes that can be learned, applied and modeled by leaders at every level."* It is possible for leaders or team members to ignore the reality of conflict. Generally, conflict is always viewed as a negative element that is simply a part of the organization. It may arise from poor communication, personality conflicts, or simply an unwillingness to cooperate.

At the end of the day the capable, developing leader recognizes that conflict is inevitable but it is also manageable and resolvable. Conflict cannot be ignored in whatever shape; form or fashion it may take. It is as simple as if we do not handle conflict, conflict will handle us.

QUESTIONS FOR REFLECTION

1. Think about a situation that you were involved in where conflict was not handled particularly well. Which model presented in this chapter would you recommend and how would you incorporate that model in a similar recent experience with conflict?

2. Which of the conflict models best identifies with the model that you currently use and if that model can be improved, how would you improve it utilizing additional principles from this chapter?

3. Smallbusiness.com says that there is both *healthy and unhealthy conflict*. Utilizing principles from this chapter, what approach would you use to minimize the potential of unhealthy conflict in your organization?

4. It has been suggested that the two major causes of conflict are *poor communication* or the *inability to control one's emotions*. Define the relationship between the two and create a plan for resolving both in your organization.

5. There are eight distinct social principles or precepts for development suggested in the Emotional Intelligence (EQ) model in this session. Which three of the eight suggested if

you implemented them today would make the most significant impact upon your team and how would you implement your selections into your organization?

QUOTES OF PRINCIPLED LEADERS

"Conflict is inevitable, but combat is optional."

Max Lucado

"The most intense conflicts, if overcome, leave behind a sense of security and calm that is not easily disturbed. It is just these intense conflicts and their conflagration which are needed to produce valuable and lasting results."

Carl Gustav Jung

"The signs of outstanding leadership appear primarily among the followers. Are the followers reaching their potential? Are they learning? Serving? Do they achieve the required results? Do they change with grace? Manage conflict?"

Max De Pree

"The hottest place in Hell is reserved for those who remain neutral in times of great moral conflict."

Martin Luther King

ESTABLISHING VALUES THAT UNITE AN ORGANIZATION

"If we ever forget that we are one Nation under God, then we will be a nation gone under."

Ronald Reagan

Foundation

In his Memorandum to All Army Leaders, General Dennis J. Reimer stated that, *"While much has changed, it's important also to recognize that there are cornerstones to our solid foundation which will never change. Finally, and probably most importantly, is* **the importance of values to our organization. Our seven inherent values--duty, honor, courage, integrity, loyalty, respect, selfless service--are what make our profession different.** *. . . . Our professional code must be those values. We must adhere to them, and instill them in our subordinates. Our job is not done until that is accomplished. Again, this is leadership by example and I expect that to happen at all levels. We will spend more time in initial entry training educating our* *recruits on the tradition and history of the United States Army and the importance of values. But one shot is not enough. We must have a sustained program in the field and it must be more than just classroom instruction. **We must make values come alive for all soldiers.***"[38]

At the time of this writing, the Army Budget Office, Washington D.C., reflects for fiscal year 2015, 490,000 soldiers for the active component, 354,200 to 350,200 for the National Guard and 202,000 to 205,000 soldiers for the Army Reserve. As the Army's most senior soldier, it was General Reimer's aim to make the inherent values of the Army *"come alive"* to over 1 million men and women that make up our Army's total current strength.

What General Reimer championed in his tenure as the 33rd Chief of Staff of the Army from June 1995-June 1999, is just as critical and relevant for leader development both in the military and civilian sectors of our society today.[39]

The Seven Army Values are a part of the bedrock foundation of soldier and leader development that becomes the catalysts for uniting personnel of the U.S. Army around the world. There are more than 150 different career paths in the Army. Once a soldier

[38] Reimer, Dennis J. Memorandum For All Army Leaders. (Washington, D.C.: Department of the Army, July 21, 1997).
[39] Editor, James J Carfano, Dennis J. Reimer. Soldiers Are Our Credentials. The Collected Works and Selected Papers of The 33rd Chief of Staff, United States Army, CMH Publishers, 2000.

qualifies, they are able to choose jobs in the fields of aviation, communications, computer sciences, medical services, engineering, infantry, law and many more.[40] What each of these 150 diverse career paths have in common are the Seven Army Values which are:

- *Loyalty* - Bear true faith and allegiance to the U.S. Constitution, the Army, your unit, and other Soldiers.
- *Duty* - Fulfill your obligations, even if it calls for sacrifice.
- *Respect* - Treat people as they should be treated.
- *Selfless Service* - Sacrifice your welfare, and your life if need be, for that of the Republic, the Army, and your subordinates.
- *Honor* - Live up to the code of a U.S. Army Soldier.
- *Integrity* - Do what's right, legally and morally.
- *Personal Courage* - Face danger, adversity or death with steadfast bravery.

The very brief definitions of each value is the platform for beginning the conversation of meaning and inculcation for soldier and leader development. The values are arranged to form the acronym *"LDRSHIP"* (leadership).

As a former ethics instructor at the United States Army and Armor Center, Fort Knox Kentucky in

---

[40] www.goarmy.com/careers-and-jobs.html. Accessed February 8, 2015.

the late 1990s, I had the privilege of teaching these values to soldiers. At that time, the audience was leaders attending the Armor Officer Basic Course, the Captains Advanced Course and twice a year, Battalion Commanders. These 3 groups of leaders attending school at the Armor Center represented progressive levels of leadership development.

As it is with any leader development program, continued progression as a leader is a must. It is from this premise that we approach this session of Ethnos Leadership. Just as the Seven Army Values have become a part of the foundation for uniting a diverse Army work force in the U.S. Army, so are they capable of uniting a work force in a public school system, restaurant or super market chain. The Cambridge Dictionary define values as *"the beliefs people have about what is right and wrong and what is most important in life, that controls behavior."*

Additionally, values are important and lasting beliefs or ideals shared by the members of a culture about what is good or bad, desirable or undesirable. Values serve as broad guidelines in all situations and are vital to the success of any organization.

The idea and aim of this chapter is to review and interpret the Seven Army Values as a means of establishing a core set of values that when applied creates uncommon, extraordinary *"**LDRSHIP**"* across any and every organizational structure.

PART I: THE VALUE OF LOYALTY

*"Everybody wants loyalty, consistency and somebody who won't quit. But everybody forgets that to **get that type of person** you have to **be that person**."*

Unknown

Every company or organization inherently desires loyalty from team members or employees.

However, sometimes what goes missing from the daily routine is the fact that in order to have loyalty from team members, the leaders must be loyal to the team members.

Loyalty becomes a motivating factor in productivity of the company. When loyalty as a value takes center stage in the nature of the organization, team members or employees go beyond the motivation of simply their paycheck. Authentic loyalty creates a sense of unity or we're all in this together. Loyalty further creates a sense of caring for and ensuring personal well-being that will help to produce organizational success. If an organization desires the value of loyalty, then every leader in the organization must become an example of loyalty.

Army Value of Loyalty-*"Bear true faith and allegiance to the U.S. Constitution, the Army, your unit and other Soldiers."* Interpreting this first value for organizationally begins with believing in and devoting yourself to the company and the members of the team.

A loyal team member or employee is one who supports the company leadership and stands up for fellow team members. Loyalty is further defined as faithfulness to commitments or obligations. It also carries the idea of a sense of duty or of devoted attachment to something or someone. When fostered and accentuated, loyalty becomes an internal sentiment or devotion that one holds for one's family, friends and organization. Loyalty is not something that is simply given, it must be earned.

When companies or organizations create environments of loyalty as a standard, team members or employees will promulgate this value across their respective departments.

Synonyms such as fidelity implies an unwavering allegiance to a person, principle or ideal. The additional synonyms of constancy, truthfulness, true-heartedness, single-mindedness, reliability, trustworthiness, dependability, submission, honesty, integrity and uprightness all reinforce the scope or the depth of this value of loyalty. The ideal of loyalty as a character trait is always guided in its conduct and actions by its devoted attachment to organizational leadership and members of the team. Loyalty always has a purpose and is always sure and never unsure concerning its aim.

The aim of the samurai of ancient Japan was to live by a code of conduct that came to be known as Bushido.

The word *"samurai"* roughly translates to *"one who serves."*[41] From the life of a samurai arose "Bushido," or the samurai code of behavior; how chivalrous men should act in their personal and professional lives. The core values of loyalty, honor and respect are three of eight virtues (values) of Bushido and the Japanese would do nothing to shame or dishonor these core values. Loyalty in Bushido to a superior was the first and most distinctive virtue of the feudal era.

The ideal was that personal fidelity was to exist amongst all honorable samurai and loyalty assumed paramount importance.[42] The feudal era eventually came to an end in 1868, and the samurai class was abolished a few years afterwards, yet Bushido is still alive in modern day Japan.[43] Considering organizational loyalty as in the samurai code of Bushido, William Shakespeare once said, *"I will follow thee to the last breath with truth and loyalty."* Creating this type of organizational loyalty can only occur by building *trust* and *truth* in those that follow you. I will never forget a 10-minute graduation speech at the United States Army and Armor Center and School, Fort Knox Kentucky in the late 1990s. The graduation

---

[41] www.pbs.org/wgbh/sugihara/readings/bushido.html. Accessed February 10, 2015.

[42] http://www.artofmanliness.com/2008/09/14/the-bushido-code-the-eight-virtues-of-the-samurai/. Accessed February 10, 2015.

[43] http://www.kendo.com/themodernsamurai. Accessed February 11, 2015.

speaker was a retired Vietnam era Major General. A soft-spoken leader, yet his presence and demeanor commanded our attention in the auditorium as he spoke. One portion of his graduation speech to the graduating class of Armor second lieutenants was as follows: *"if your soldiers trust you they will charge hell with an empty water pistol for you."* When a leader has imparted by word and deed, trust and truth in their employee's, the loyalty of the organization will follow. When leaders prove that every team member or employee is valuable, they are willing to sacrifice because organizational honesty and integrity can be trusted.

This does not mean that the leader has to get everything right, because an established *"truth and trust account"* will cover any mistakes that a leader may make. This is where and how uncommon loyalty can be established both as a value and valuable to those that follow.

Part II: The Value of Duty

. . . .

"Don't waste life in doubts and fears; spend yourself on the work before you, well assured that the right performance of this hour's duties will be the best preparation for the hours and ages that will follow it."

Ralph Waldo Emerson

Army Value of Duty-*Fulfill your obligations.* Doing your duty means more than carrying out your assigned tasks. Duty means being able to accomplish tasks as part of a team. The work of the U.S. Army is a complex combination of missions, tasks and responsibilities — all in constant motion. Our work entails building one assignment onto another. You fulfill your obligations as a part of your unit every time you resist the temptation to take "shortcuts" that might undermine the integrity of the final product.[44]

Every company or organization is in operation to serve a need to their community and to be profitable. If the company is not profitable they will not be in business for long.

John D. Rockefeller, Jr. stated that, *"I believe that the rendering of useful service is the common duty of mankind and that only in the purifying fire of sacrifice is the dross of selfishness consumed and the greatness of the human*

---

[44] http://www.army.mil/values/. Accessed February 11, 2015.

soul set free."[45] Rockefeller Jr. was a philanthropist who gave more than $537 million to educational organizations, religious causes, hospitals, scientific projects, conservation and parklands, and historic preservation and other charitable projects. The son of John D. Rockefeller, founder of the Standard Oil Company, and Laura Spelman Rockefeller, he was born in Cleveland, Ohio, on January 29, 1874, and died in Tucson, Arizona, on May 11, 1960.

He was responsible for the restoration of Colonial Williamsburg in Virginia, and he donated the land along the East River in Manhattan for the site of the United Nations Headquarters. Imbued with a deep sense of stewardship, John D. Rockefeller, Jr. believed that his inherited fortune should be used for the public good.[46] One does not act have to be a multimillionaire to operate personally and professionally from the position of duty (responsibility). John D. Rockefeller Jr.'s inheritance left him with a deep sense of stewardship. In this sense, we can rightly conclude that he believed that he had a duty as a philanthropist for the common good.

When Emerson stated, *"don't waste life in doubts and fears; spend yourself on the work before you, well assured that the right performance of this hour's duties will be the best preparation for the hours and ages that will follow it,"*

---

[45] http://www.rockarch.org/bio/jdrjr.php. Accessed February 11, 2015.

[46] IBID, Accessed February 11, 2015.

carries in essence the same meaning as Rockefeller's philanthropic position of "the common good."

A basic definition from Merriam Webster's Dictionary of duty is *"obligatory tasks, conduct, service, or functions that arise from one's position."* As a team member or employee every day is a new opportunity to fulfill the functions and tasks that are expected based on one's position. In the military, if one does not do his or her duty, it has the potential of costing someone their life on the battlefield.

Within the company, if one does not do his or her duty, it has the potential of causing the loss of money. If the company or organization begins to lose money, the consequences may be reductions in the workforce, or the loss of jobs. The loss of jobs affects families and communities that ultimately affects our nation. When we spend or invest our life in the work, the duty that is before us is as Emerson stated; it is *"in preparation for our future."* As a grandfather with eight grandchildren, there is not a day that does not go by that I do not think about their future. There is a duty that we have to our families, there is a duty that we have to our communities, and there is a duty that we have to our nation as responsible adult citizens.

If we lose sight of our duty to one another what kind of world will we leave behind for our children and our children's children? The principle of duty is more than *"obligatory tasks, conduct, service, or functions that arise from one's position,"* when we consider the potential costs of *not* doing our duty concerning the future of our children, our grandchildren and great-grandchildren. Albert Einstein once said, *"That only a life lived for others is a life worth living."*

The only thing that is constant is change. As a leader or follower and member of the team, what is my duty to others today? There will always be constant change in our elected government officials. There will always be constant change in our military leadership and within our companies and organizations in our nation. Yet, the principle of duty will always remain the same. The Army defines value from the place of fulfilling your obligations. From this definition, doing your duty means more than carrying out assigned tasks. Duty means being able to accomplish tasks as part of a team.

Whether leader or follower, what we do with the life that we live contributes to someone's future because whatever endeavors we have, we are connected as a team. This certainly begins with our families and when we understand our duty, it ought to carry over to our coworkers. This is the essence of mentorship.

Purposeful relationships with others, that gains authentic accountability, which ultimately becomes my professional responsibility. It is recognizing that each one of us has the potential to make a positive difference in someone's life and it is my duty to do so. It is from this mindset that Rockefeller's thoughts of, *"useful service is the common duty of mankind…and by the purifying fire of sacrifice is the dross of selfishness consumed,"* that duty becomes a synergetic stimulus for making a difference that counts for future generations.

PART III: THE VALUE OF RESPECT

"Show respect even to people who don't deserve it; not as a reflection of their character, but as a reflection of yours."
Dave Willis

To respect someone is to give esteem or honor normally due to admirable qualities that a person exhibits. The Army Value of Respect states that we are to: ***"Treat people as they should be treated."*** Further defined in the Soldier's Code, soldiers pledge to treat others with dignity and respect while expecting others to do the same. According to the Army's definition, respect is what allows soldiers to appreciate the best in other people. Respect is trusting that all people have done their jobs and fulfilled their duty.

And self-respect is a vital ingredient with the Army value of respect, which results from knowing you have put forth your best effort. The Army is one team and each of us has something to contribute.[47]

A short story entitled *"Night Watch"* written by Roy Popkins in 1964 very powerfully portrays the impact that this principle of respect or the precept of *"treat people as they should be treated"* communicates. The story tells of the night that a young Marine entered a hospital and as soon as the nurse saw him, she took him immediately to the bedside of an old dying man

---

[47] http://www.army.mil/values/. Accessed February 13, 2015.

and told him, your son is here. The old man gripped the hand of the young Marine very tightly and simply held on throughout the night. The nurse could hear the young Marine whispering words of encouragement throughout the night as he held onto the man's hand. Early the next morning, the old man died. The Marine went to find the nurse and asked her the name of the old man. Responding with surprise the nurse said, He was your father and you don't know his name? The young Marine responded I have never seen that man before in my life, he was not my father. I knew that a mistake had been made the moment that you brought me into his room. I understood that he needed his son, and his son was not here, so I decided to stay.[48]

The young Marine in this story treated this dying man as he should have been treated. To respect someone is to give esteem or honor to someone. As members of any organizational team treating each other as they should be treated is related to what many know as the *"Golden Rule." "Do unto others as you would have them do unto you."* What some may not know is that this principle or rule is motivated by love. The Marine in the story did not know the dying man, however what is evident is that this dying man needed the love of his son and this duty bound Marine treated him as he should have been treated. C.S. Lewis once said, *"To love at all is to be vulnerable."*

---

[48] http://www.thinkingagain.com/html/nightwatch.html. Accessed November 22, 2015.

To speak of love in the workplace is uncommon due to apprehensions or fears of being misunderstood.

Yet, on our football fields, our baseball stadiums and basketball arenas when championships are won, players embrace one another with expressions of gratitude and appreciation for one another for their contributions to the team. Without hesitation the Marine in Popkins story was not only *vulnerable*, but he was also *available* to express gratitude and appreciation, rooted in love, for a dying man that he did not know. Love is compassion in action. To establish a value such as treating others as they should be treated is the responsibility (duty) of every member of the team. At the end of the day, *every day*, our ability to respect one another is not a reflection of someone else's character it is a reflection of our own.

PART IV: THE VALUE OF SELFLESS SERVICE

....

"Only a life lived for others is a life worth living."
                                        Albert Einstein

The Army Value of Selfless Service means to **"put the welfare of the Nation, the Army and your subordinates before your own."** Selfless service is larger than just one person. It is to remind soldiers that in serving your country, you are doing your duty loyally without thought of recognition or gain. The basic building block of selfless service is the commitment of each team member to go a little further, endure a little longer, and look a little closer to see how he or she can add to the effort.[49] When we look at the essence of former President Ronald Reagan's comments concerning the *"willingness of our citizens to give freely and unselfishly of themselves,"* this is the place where selfless service begins.

To be willing is simply a matter of one's will. In this sense, will is defined as *"the power of choosing one's own actions."*[50] H. Burke Peterson says that, *"a selfless person is one who is more concerned about the happiness and well-being of another than about his or her own convenience or comfort, one who is willing to serve another when it is*

---

[49] http://www.army.mil/values/. Accessed February 13, 2015.
[50] www.dictionary.com. Accessed February 14, 2015.

neither sought for nor appreciated, or one who is willing to serve even those whom he or she dislikes.

A selfless person displays a willingness to sacrifice, a willingness to put aside personal wants, and needs, and feelings."[51] Doug Moran in his article entitled, *"Selfless Leadership: Putting Our Cause First"* lists 4 ways that a leader or team member can become more selfless.

- *Subordinate our personal feelings/needs/ego to the greater good.* When we commit ourselves to a cause, we will often need to put the cause ahead of our personal goals for the greater good of the organization or the team.
- *Selflessness takes practice.* We can't just wake up one morning and become selfless leaders. It takes practice and discipline. Selflessness often goes against our natural instincts for self-preservation. It requires us to build and exercise new muscles. We have to look for opportunities, both big and small, to practice selflessness.
- *Don't confuse selflessness with a lack of will or sense of self.* Many may confuse selflessness with weakness or lack of will. On the contrary, selfless leaders often have huge egos and make the choice to sacrifice for the organization or the cause.
- *Selflessness requires leaders to understand boundaries and priorities.* If the cause is great

---

[51] http://speeches.byu.edu/.The Power of One. Accessed February 15, 2015.

and we believe in our ability to effect change, we should be prepared to make great sacrifices as needed. It requires the leader or team member to fully explore our boundaries (family, time, promotions, etc.) so that when we confront choices we are prepared to make them for the good of the organization.[52]

Moran concludes his article by stating that, *"anyone can become a selfless leader. Selfless leadership requires hard work, patience, sacrifice, and most of all love. We must love what we do, the people we serve, and our cause."*[53] Martin Luther King once stated that, *"Life's most persistent and urgent question is, what are you doing for others?"* To answer Dr. King's question from an organizational perspective, when we do for others, it is *our choice* that we do for others. It is a thinking of *self-less* and thinking of *others* more. In so doing, either as a leader or team member, we become tangible proof and evidence of *"love of what we do, the people that we serve and the cause in which we believe."*

[52] http://www.strategydriven.com/2010/11/22/selfless-leadership-putting-our-cause-first/. Accessed February 15, 2015.
[53] http://www.strategydriven.com/2010/11/22/selfless-leadership-putting-our-cause-first/. Accessed February 15, 2015.

PART V: THE VALUE OF HONOR

· ·

"The purpose of life is not to be happy. It is to be useful, to be honorable, to be compassionate, to have it make some difference that you have lived and lived well."

Ralph Waldo Emerson

<u>**Army Value of Honor:**</u> *"**Live up to Army values.**"* The Nation's highest military award is The Medal of Honor. This award goes to soldiers who make honor a matter of daily living — soldiers who develop the habit of being honorable, and solidify that habit with every value choice they make. Honor is a matter of carrying out, acting, and living the values of respect, duty, loyalty, selfless service, integrity and personal courage in everything you do.[54] The value of honor further means *"respect and esteem shown to another."*

In addition to the preceding, honor is also the *"recognition of one's right to great respect or to any expression of such recognition."* The word deference also fosters the essence of the ideal of honor. The word deference indicates *"a profound respect interwoven with love and devotion."*[55]

Over 20 years ago the *"Honorable CHARACTER Classroom Management System"* was created by teachers for teachers for the purpose of training students in

---

[54] http://www.army.mil/values/. Accessed February 15, 2015.
[55] www.dictionary.com. Accessed February 15, 2015.

honorable character living. Each classroom maintains charts that have fourteen honorable characteristics listed on it.

Respect, obedience, diligence, wisdom, kindness, self-control, orderliness, service, attentiveness, cooperation, courage, honesty, forgiveness, and responsibility are what the teachers are looking for in each student. It is monitored by both teacher and students. Rewards from the positive reinforcement of the fourteen traits from both the teacher and classmates has proven to improve behavior of even those students that have struggled behaviorally.[56]

The central theme of the program is much like that of the Seven Army Values of loyalty, duty, respect, selfless service, honor, integrity and personal courage. The teachers that created the *Honorable Character Classroom Management System* over 20 years ago recognized the importance of a values based approach in their classrooms that would assist in producing desired behavior in their students.

As stated earlier, honor is *"respect and esteem shown to another."* Honor is also the *"recognition of one's right to great respect or to any expression of such recognition."* The objective of the Seven Army Values, and The Honorable Character Classroom Management System, is to create an organizational atmosphere and environment of honorable living that leads to

---

[56] http://www.honorablecharacter.com/faq. Accessed February 15, 2015.

responsible citizenship. Every person is worthy of great respect and recognition of the same.

In any organizational structure, when team members or leaders are honored and value the results will be seen in the attitude that the team displays.

Dr. Ed Brenegar in an article entitled, "To Live Honorably Is To Recognize How We Are Connected Together," says that, *"living honorably is an aspect of living with gratitude. Much of what passes for gratitude today is a psychological elixir to make one feel good. It is a self-referential act rather than a self-giving or even a sacrificial one. To honor others is to stand before each human being we encounter with the attitude that they are worthy of dignity, respect, and honor as human beings. Honor is an integral part of leadership."* [57] Brenegar also states that, *"the tradition of honor extends back to the time of Homer and the ancient Greeks. Honor was a dedication to the higher ideals of community and national allegiance. To live with honor was the recognition that I am not simply my own, but owe gratitude and service to my community."*[58] A community that shares the value of honor with each other understands that they are respected not only individually, but this philosophy also promotes corporate unity. Subsequently, this creates a reality for every team member that I am personally valuable.

---

[57] http://edbrenegar.typepad.com/leading_questions/2009/07/observations-on-the-path-to-an-honorable-life. Accessed February 15, 2015.

[58] IBID. Accessed February 15, 2015.

This ethos further builds within the organization a solidarity that establishes loyalty and unity that will ultimately increase productivity because of the honor that is given to each member of the team. When Ralph Waldo Emerson wrote that, *"The purpose of life is not to be happy. It is to be useful, to be honorable, to be compassionate, to have it make some difference that you have lived and lived well."* This is certainly a profound expression from Mr. Emerson. However, I submit that when you have lived your life well, happiness will also follow. As an honorable leader or team member, there is an intrinsic satisfaction of knowing as others have said, "job well done." I have made a difference and I have done so because of honor that was given to others.

PART VI: THE VALUE OF INTEGRITY

....

"Look for 3 things in a person. Intelligence, energy and integrity. If they don't have the last one, don't even bother with the first two."

Warren Buffet

The Army Value of Integrity says, ***"do what's right, legally and morally."*** The Army definition of integrity further says that it is a quality you develop by adhering to moral principles. It requires that you do and say nothing that deceives others. As your integrity grows, so does the trust others place in you.

The more choices you make based on integrity, the more this highly prized value will affect your relationships with family and friends, and, finally, the fundamental acceptance of yourself.[59] In the book *"The Character-Based Leader,"* one of the authors Susan Mazza states that, *"there are two essential dimensions of personal integrity: **authenticity and accountability.*** As a character based leader, Mazza also state's that *"when you're being authentic, your words and actions are aligned with each other. Additionally, both your words and actions are aligned with your beliefs and commitments. Authenticity requires that you are true to yourself."* The second dimension is that of accountability. To be

---

[59] http://www.army.mil/values/. Accessed February 15, 2015.

accountable is to *"make a promise to another with a commitment to honor that promise."*[60]

At its most basic level, integrity is about being true to our personal beliefs, values and principles. From this perspective the discussion of integrity begins with the personal inquiry into what values and principles each of us will use as the guide for our behavior and conduct. The American Heritage Dictionary defines integrity as, *"steadfast adherence to a strict moral code or strong moral principles that one refuses to change."* An example of a strict code of ethics is the Cadet Honor Code that has been in the foundation of the United States Military Academy, West Point since 1947.[61]

The Cadet Honor Code simply states that, *"A cadet will not lie, cheat or steal or tolerate those that do."* The Cadet Honor Code communicates the standards of integrity expected of all West Point Cadets and graduates. It is the means through which we are able to apply the ethical ideal, honorable living, to our lives.[62]

Mazza says that, *"once a person declares their personal code of ethics, that person consciously enters into an accountable relationship."* An accountable relationship is one that is valued, trusted and respected.

---

[60] Lead Change Group, Inc. The Character Based Leader. Indianapolis: Dog Ear Publishing, 2012, pg.73.
[61] http://en.wikipedia.org/wiki/Cadet_Honor_Code. Accessed February 15, 2015.
[62] http://www.west-point.org/publications/honorsys/chap1. html. Accessed February 15, 2015.

Accountability also carries a mindset of responsible answerability concerning actions, conduct and behavior; the right and the wrong. In these trusted and respected relationships leaders understand that no matter the level of leadership I achieve, humility and integrity compels me to be accountable. In a blog written for the Washington Post, Colonel Eric Kail, course director of military leadership at the U.S. Military Academy at West Point says that there are two critical components of integrity that go beyond just doing the right thing when no one is looking:

> "The first is the **adherence to a moral or ethical principle** *which is not simple compliance to rules. What is implied is a philosophical understanding of the reason it exists.*
>
> *Secondly, Kail states that it is* **the pursuit of an undiminished state or condition of integrity.**" [63]

A moral code is comprised of the principles, values, and beliefs that become our leadership guide for life. An allegiance and dedication to *"choosing the harder right instead of the easier wrong"* assists in the establishment for uncompromising leadership.

---

[63] http://www.washingtonpost.com/blogs/guest-insights/post/leadership-character-the-role-of-integrity/2011/04/04/. Accessed February 16, 2015.

DR. GREGORY L. CRUELL

In other words, as a leader of uncompromising integrity, one's conduct and behavior is governed by one's solidified morality. Kail's position of a continual pursuit of an undiminished state of integrity suggests and encourages an endless quest of development of what may be the most critical character attribute of all for the greater good of all.

Additional insight into the cultivation of one's character and integrity is further affirmed by the ancient Greek philosopher Heraclitus. *"The soul is dyed the color of its thoughts. Think only on most things that are in line with your principles and can bear the light of day. The content of your character is your choice. Day by day, what you do is who you become. Your integrity is your destiny, it is a light to guide your way."*[64]

If Heraclitus is correct, what holds everything (personally and organizationally) together is a persistent pursuit of one's leadership destiny though integrity (wholeness and completeness).

---

[64] www.quotatio.com. Accessed February 16, 2015.

Part VII: The Value of Personal Courage

....

"Courage is not the absence of fear, but rather the judgment that something else is more important."

Ambrose Redmon

The Oxford English dictionary says that, *"morals are concerned with a person standards of behaviors or beliefs concerning what is and is not acceptable for them to do."* The Army Value of Personal Courage is defined as the ability to *"face fear, danger or adversity (physical or moral)."* With physical courage, it is a matter of enduring physical duress and at times risking personal safety. Facing moral fear or adversity may be a long, slow process of continuing forward on the right path, especially if taking those actions is not popular with others.

You can build your personal courage by daily standing up for and acting upon the things that you know are honorable.[65] Our military personnel, our local fire fighters, police departments, and emergency services personnel must face unknown circumstances and are challenged to live by this value of personal courage daily.

The world and society in which we live is a very dangerous place and there are many other examples

---

[65] http://www.army.mil/values/. Accessed February 16, 2015.

of physical and moral courage that encourage and inspire.

This type of courage comes in many shapes, sizes and forms. Running into a burning building to help save lives or coming to the aid of a person that is being robbed or assaulted are certainly courageous and admirable acts. Yet courage can also be seen in confronting a bully at school or asking out a secret crush out on a date both require certain levels of bravery. Therefore, acts full of courage can happen on a very large public scale, but also on the smaller, more private day to day life level. Day to day life examples like:

- Standing up for yourself.
- Leaving an abusive relationship.
- Standing up for someone that is being abused.
- Taking a stand against an unfair social or economic practice in the organization.
- Standing up against racism or prejudice.
- Leaving a job that you don't like and moving forward to find a new one.

Physical and moral courage also includes the story of former law enforcement officer Bobby Smith. On the night of March 14, 1986, at point blank range, Bobby Smith was shot in the face & blinded by an armed, violent drug offender.

Bobby had been a law enforcement officer in Louisiana for nine years at the time of this brutal act against his life. He recalls lying face down on the center lane of the highway, soaked in blood, and thinking, *"Will this be the day that I die?"* But Bobby chose to not give up; he chose not to die that day; he chose to fight and live. The days, weeks, and even years following the trauma were filled with many fears about his future, daily struggles adjusting to blindness, and financial hardships. Bobby had lost his eyesight, career, self-confidence, independence, and marriage. Then tragically, in 1997, Bobby's daughter, Kim, was killed at 22 years old in an automobile accident. Yet today, Bobby Smith declares that the losses in his life have been his catalyst for life. Bobby believes that his life is not defined by the losses that he has endured and triumphed over. No, he believes that his defining moment, and ours too, comes every morning when we rise, face the challenges of the day, no matter what they are and decide that *today I choose to live.* [66] Bobby Smith's decision to choose to live after horrendous and tragic life circumstances is a daily act of personal courage.

Helen Keller once stated that, *"the greatest tragedy in the world is to have sight and not be able to see."* The life of this former police officer Bobby Smith, personifies the revelation and insight that the also blind author and political activist Helen Keller declared many years ago.

---

[66] http://www.visionsofcourage.com/. Accessed February 16, 2015.

Through tragic life circumstances, Mr. Smith could "*see*," although blinded by an armed violent drug offender that I still have choices and I choose to live, which is a personal act of courage. Just as we are inspired by physical acts of courage, moral courage is equally esteemed as a part of the value of personal courage.

In the journal, "*Business Ethics: European Review 2007*," Leslie E. Sekerka and Richard P. Bagozzin contribute an article entitled, *"Moral Courage in The Workplace: Moving To and From The Desire and Decision To Act."* In this journal, the authors define moral courage as, *"the ability to use inner principles to do what is good for others, regardless of threat to self, as a matter of practice. We believe that this involves the conscious reflection on one's desires to act, or the lack of such a desire thereof, as one moves towards engagement. How a person goes about resolving the conflicts between their desires and personal standards is what ultimately leads to a decision to engage in morally courageous behavior."* [67]In 2004, Ethics Resource Center staff member Rielle Miller wrote a white paper entitled, *"Moral Courage: Definition and Development.* In the conclusion of her research Miller states, *"to develop moral courage, moral courage must be habituated and practiced. Moral courage is one of those*

---

[67] Leslie E. Sekerka and Richard P. Bagozzin. Moral Courage in The Workplace: Moving To and From The Desire and Decision To Act. (Malden: Blackwell Publishing), 2007.

things that can only be properly attained by doing it. To get courage, be courageous."[68]

In Rielle Millers, Leslie E. Sekerka and Richard P. Bagozzin's contribution to this section concerning moral courage, a common theme emerges. It is the recognition of a *moral situation, and a decision to act upon the situation.* The emergent theme also suggests that in order to be a person of moral courage it must be practiced or developed for the common good, which includes *the capability to confront, to be confronted and to take action.*

Courage Requires The Capability To Confront

"You can't change what you refuse to confront."

Unknown

The capability to confront is to speak the truth, with tact and respect. Moral courage from this perspective requires a review of your core values and aspirations and as a leader what is at stake if you don't confront. This also includes confronting self. Speaking the truth is a partner of integrity. For most people confrontation is never easy, however, sometimes it is necessary for correction and instruction of a circumstance that can be potentially harmful or destructive. If there is no instruction with the correction, what you are left with is uncertainty. Is this situation right or is it wrong?

---

[68] Miller, Rielle. Moral Courage: Definition and Development. Ethics Resource Center, Arlington, 2005.

When truth is spoken and correction with instruction is given, with tact and respect, the outcome always lends itself to the positive.

Courage Requires The Capability To Be Confronted

"We have to confront ourselves. Do we like what we see in the mirror? And according to our courage we will have to say yea or nay-and rise!

Adapted From Maya Angelou

Vocabulary.Com defines criticism as a noun most often used to describe *"negative commentary about something or someone."* In addition, criticism also means *"an examination or judgment of a matter or situation."* One derivation of its original root word *critic* in Greek is *"krino."*

Which means to properly separate, distinguish, judge, or come to a choice by making a judgment – either positive (a verdict in favor of) or negative (which rejects or condemns).[69]

Criticism is most often viewed from a negative perspective rather than from a positive one. The moral courage to be confronted is critical to true integrity. This allows the leader to learn from the insights, criticisms, and challenges of others, and enables necessary course corrections in leadership. Instead of

[69] http://biblehub.com/greek/2919.htm. Accessed October 25, 2015.

reacting to criticism as an attack, the criticism itself can be a benevolent instructor. The capability to be confronted incudes having trusted co-workers that can help you to evaluate the criticism. The point is that criticism does not always have to be received negatively. It can work *positively* for development. This includes giving up the need to be right.

Determine to learn from others when criticized or confronted you. The only barriers to learning are the scar tissues of our own egos, caused by bad work or leadership experiences. Leave the past in the past and move forward. Take each criticism as an opportunity to be the student of criticism, to learn more about yourself and the workings of your own mind and heart. Listen and learn with an open heart.

In the final analysis of developing the capability to be confronted, as much as I may believe that I am right, I could also be wrong.

Courage Requires The Capability To Take Action

In April of 2014, Deborah Hughes, 59, of Detroit, had the courage to act and saved the life of Steve Utash. Steve had accidently hit a 10 year old boy with his truck and as he got out of his truck to help the boy, he was attacked and was being beaten by a mob that had quickly gathered at the scene of the accident. Deborah first checked on the child and while comforting the boy, she looked up and saw a mob nearby, beating a man.

Deborah made her way through the crowd and used her own body as a human shield for Utash and pleaded with the crowd, *"Please don't kick him no more ... please don't hit him, don't do it,"* she recalled saying. The crowd started backing up. Hughes performed CPR on Utash and no one stopped or tried to hurt her. The ambulance arrived. Deborah said although she was scared, fear did not stop her. *"I don't know. Something happened. I had courage. I just didn't want them to hurt him,"* she said in a December interview with the Free Press. *"Sometimes, I'll sit here and I'll cry. And I'll say, 'Did I actually do that?'"* Hughes, however, is certain of one thing.

If she had not stepped in to intervene, she said: *"He would be dead ... those boys would have beat him to death."*[70] The courage to take action is the willingness to place yourself in harm's way. It is a willingness to move towards the conflict. Whether it be moral or physical. It is important to note that whatever we choose, every decision has consequences.

Had Deborah decided *not* to act on the behalf of a man that she did not know, Utash most likely would not have survived. Deborah Hughes at 4"11 and 126 pounds *did* choose to act that day which saved the life of Steve Utash. At 59 years old, Deborah had not planned to be a heroine on the morning of April 8th, 2014 and yet her life validates that hero's and heroine's

---

[70] http://www.detroitnews.com/article/20140408/ METRO01/304080026. Accessed October 25, 2015.

come in all shapes, sizes and professions. Perhaps for Deborah it was instinct or an internal moral compass that caused her to act courageously and in so doing, became a heroine that the Utash family will never forget.

The intent of this session was to consider the U.S. Army's Seven Values (LDRSHIP) with additional insight from other sources for possible inclusion in any work environment for the purpose of establishing unity in any organization.

The ethos that all soldiers share are these Seven Army Values that are intended to unite our Army with a common mindset for leadership. Our belief at Ethnos Leadership is that these values will accomplish the same goal in any organization when intentionally and purposely applied.

Although people come from different cultures and environments, for any organization to be successful, there must be values that unite us personally and as this is accomplished, greater success organizationally will become our reality.

SUMMATION: ESTABLISHING VALUES THAT UNITE AN ORGANIZATION

The Seven Army Values are a part of the bedrock foundation of soldier and leader development that becomes the catalysts for uniting personnel of the U.S. Army around the world. There are more than 150 different career paths in the Army.

Once a soldier qualifies, they are able to choose jobs in the fields of aviation, communications, computer sciences, medical services, engineering, infantry, law and many more.[71] What each of these 150 diverse career paths have in common are the Seven Army Values which are:

- *Loyalty* - Bear true faith and allegiance to the U.S. Constitution, the Army, your unit, and other Soldiers.
- *Duty* - Fulfill your obligations, even if it calls for sacrifice.
- *Respect* - Treat people as they should be treated.
- *Selfless Service* - Sacrifice your welfare, and your life if need be, for that of the Republic, the Army, and your subordinates.
- *Honor* - Live up to the code of a U.S. Army Soldier.

---

[71] www.goarmy.com/careers-and-jobs.html. Accessed February 8, 2015.

- *Integrity* - Do what's right, legally and morally.
- *Personal Courage* - Face danger, adversity or death with steadfast bravery.

Just as the Seven Army Values have become a part of the foundation for uniting a diverse Army work force in the U.S. Army, so are they capable of uniting a work force in a public school system, restaurant or super market chain. The Cambridge Dictionary define values as *"the beliefs people have about what is right and wrong and what is most important in life, that controls behavior."* Additionally, values are important and lasting beliefs or ideals shared by the members of a culture about what is good or bad, desirable or undesirable. Values serve as broad guidelines in all situations and are vital to the success of any organization. Living (working) by values such as the ones that have been suggested in this session creates an attitude (mindset) personally that impacts employees or team members organizationally.

From this perspective, our values become words that we live by or those principles that govern our conduct and behavior. A person that lives intentionally by principles such as the Seven Army Values becomes an agent of change and a model of what is good, right or just. What will always be respected in our society are people that hold to the standards that their values establish. These are the people, these are the leaders that make a difference and they make a difference one life at a time.

QUESTIONS FOR REFLECTION

1. How would you convince or persuade those that follow you or members of your team of the importance of living a *"value filled"* life personally and organizationally?

2. How would you rate or evaluate adherence by the leadership and employees of your organization to the values of your organization? What strategies would you suggest to senior leadership to improve organizational adherence to these values?

3. This session has suggested that values are the means of uniting an organization. Are values enough to unite an organization? Why or why not?

4. Which of the seven values presented in this session are the most valuable to you as a leader? Explain why they are the most valuable.

5. With a potential new employee or member of your team utilizing principles from this session, what questions would you create to ask in an interview to determine if this is a value filled person?

Quotes of Principled Leaders

"In a world that is divided by our racial, cultural, religious, and economic differences we exist as individuals. Instead we should examine our human similarities and realize we are all the same. We're all human and we are better together."

Unknown

"Teamwork is the ability to work together toward a common vision. The ability to direct individual accomplishment towards organizational objectives. It is the fuel that allows common people to attain uncommon results."

Successories

"There is no strength without unity."

Irish Proverb

"Coming together is a beginning, keeping it together is progress, working together is success."

Henry Ford

"We must learn to live together as brothers or we will perish together as fools."

Martin Luther King

CREATING TRANSFORMATIONAL LEADERS WHO TRANSFORM OTHERS

Foundation

"Average leaders raise the bar on themselves; good leaders raise the bar for others; great leaders inspire others to raise their own bar."

Orrin Woodward

In an article written for Forbes Magazine, Glenn Llopis states that, *"every leader must be a change agent or face extinction."* Llopis goes on to say that, *"change is difficult. Not changing is fatal."*[72] Transformational leadership is about change. The emergence of transformational leadership as a concept began with a book by the political scientist James MacGregor

---

[72] www.forbes.com/sites/glenllopis/2014/03/24/every leader must be a change agent. Accessed February 6, 2015.

Burns titled *"Leadership"* in 1978.[73] According to Burns, transformational leadership is seen and experienced when *"leaders and followers make each other to advance to a higher level of morality and motivation."*[74]

Through the strength of their vision and personality, transformational leaders are able to inspire followers to change expectations, perceptions, and motivations to work towards common goals. Burns also makes reference to Mohandas Gandhi as a classic example of transformational leadership.

Gandhi raised the hopes and expectations of millions of his people, and in the process was changed himself.[75] Transformational leadership, as the name implies is a process that changes and transforms.

It is grounded in positive change of the emotions, values, ethics, standards for the accomplishment of long-term goals of individuals and organizations. Transformational leadership is also concerned with follower's motives, satisfying their needs and incorporating their ideals into the process of transformation. It is a leadership style that can inspire positive changes in those who follow.[76]

Transformational leaders are generally energetic, enthusiastic, and passionate. This type of leader is concerned, focused and engaged in helping every

---

[73] Northouse, Peter G. Leadership Theory and Practice. Thousand Oaks, California: Sage Publications, 2004, p. 170.
[74] IBID, p. 170.
[75] IBID, p.170.
[76] IBID, p. 169.

member of the team to succeed via the process of transformational leadership.[77] Phillip V. Lewis stated that the goal of a transformational leader is to *"transform people and organizations: change minds and hearts; enlarge vision, insight, and understanding; clarify purposes; make behavior congruent with beliefs, principles, and values; and bring about changes that are permanent, self-perpetuating, and momentum building."*[78]

Bernard M. Bass expanded upon Burns' original ideas to develop what is today referred to as *"Bass' Transformational Leadership Theory."* According to Bass, transformational leadership can be defined based on the impact that it has on followers. According to Bass, transformational leaders *"earn trust, respect, and admiration from their followers"* and in essence this is what produces the transformation.[79] Bass suggests that there are four components of transformational leadership:

1. *Idealized Influence*: this component causes the transformational leader to be admired, respected and trusted. Followers identify with the leaders and want to emulate them. Leaders

---

[77] http://psychology.about.com/od/leadership/a/transformational.htm. Accessed January 21, 2015.

[78] Lewis, P. V. (1996). Transformational Leadership: A New Model for Total Church Involvement. Nashville, TN: Broadman & Holman.

[79] http://psychology.about.com/od/leadership/a/transformational.htm. Accessed January 21, 2015.

are endowed by their followers as having extraordinary capabilities, persistence and determination. These leaders are willing to take risks and are consistent rather than erratic in behavior.

They can be counted on to do the right thing, demonstrating high standards of ethical and moral conduct.[80]

2. *Inspirational Motivation*: this aspect of a transformational leader aims to motivate and inspire team members in what they do in the work environment. Team spirit is fostered and welcomed. Enthusiasm and optimism are displayed. Leaders get followers involved in envisioning the future state of the organization. This component of transformational leadership clearly communicates expectations that followers want to meet and demonstrates commitment to goals and the shared vision.[81]

3. *Intellectual Stimulation*: transformational leaders stimulate their follower's efforts to be innovative and creative by questioning assumptions, reframing problems and approaching old situations in new ways. Creativity is encouraged. Followers are encouraged to try new approaches, and their

[80] Bernard Bass and Ralph Stogdill, Handbook of Leadership, Theory, Research and Managerial Applications, 3rd Edition, (New York: The Free Press), 1990, p. 5.
[81] IBID, p. 5.

ideas are not criticized because they differ from the leader's ideas.[82]

4. ***Individualized Consideration***: transformational leaders pay special attention to each individual followers needs for achievement and growth acting as coach or mentor. Individualized consideration is practiced when new learning opportunities are created along with a supportive climate. The individually considerate leader listens intently. A two-way exchange of communication is encouraged. Interaction with followers are *personalized* and not *marginalized*.[83]

Psychologist and leadership expert Ronald E. Riggio concludes that, *evidence clearly shows that groups led by transformational leaders have higher levels of performance and satisfaction than groups led by other types of leaders*.[84] The reason, Riggio suggests, is that transformational leaders believe that their followers can do their best by inspiration and empowerment and thus, transformation occurs both personally and organizationally.[85] James MacGregor Burns' initial ideal or thought of a transformational leader is just as relevant today as it was in 1978. Burn's thought

[82] IBID, p. 5.
[83] IBID, p.5.
[84] http://psychology.about.com/od/leadership/a/transformational.htm. Accessed January 21, 2015.
[85] IBID.

of *"leaders and followers make each other to advance to a higher level of morality and motivation."*

Morality (what's right) and motivation (intrinsic incentive) serve as the cornerstone of the four components of transformational leadership: *idealized influence, inspirational motivation, intellectual stimulation,* and *individualized consideration.* As we examine the intent of this session, what is suggested is that transformational leadership serves as a valuable ally in the pursuit of transforming our organizations, and as in the case of Mohandas Gandhi, thereby transforming ourselves.

PART I: CREATING INFLUENCE THAT TRANSFORMS

. . . .

"You must be the change you wish to see in the world."
Mohandas Gandhi

It is important to note that at the outset of this session as we discuss creating a transformational leader, that none of us are perfect. In addition to this, when we are completely honest, most will acknowledge that we are *far* from being perfect!

Thus, from the very outset, transformational leadership in some respects, undergirds the fact that leadership is not a destination, it is a journey. In fact, many would agree that leadership is a *lifelong journey of learning*. In order to create a transformational leader one must first admit or knowledge that I need to be transformed.

This acknowledgment requires an uncommon leadership trait known as humility. As we expand upon Bass's definition of idealized influence, the point of humility is that a transformational leader is secure enough to recognize his or her weaknesses and to seek the input and talents of others. By being receptive to outside ideas and assistance, they open up new avenues for the organization and for those that follow them. For the purposes of this session humility simply means, *"Not proud or arrogant, one that is courteously respectful."*[86]

Humility many times is seen as *"weakness"* rather than *"meekness"*; which is modesty or power under control. In his book, *The One Minute Manager,* Ken Blanchard states *"People with humility do not think less of themselves; they just think about themselves less."*[87]

According to Jim Collins in his book *"Good To Great,"* humility and modesty are key ingredients of Level 5 leadership (which is also transformational). This type of leader embodies personal humility and the professional will to do whatever it takes to get results with modesty and self-efficacy. This attribute of humility is not weakness, it is meekness, which is strength under control. These types of capable leaders have an unshakeable resolve and drive to make the people around them, and the organization to which they belong great. [88]

Although it goes against the norm of our society and the teachings that we've learned, the development of humility can help us cut through and overcome most conflicts and obstacles and help us create harmonious situations in our personal and organizational lives.

---

[86] www.dictionary.com. Accessed January 30, 2015.

[87] http://www.huffingtonpost.com/gadadhara-pandit-dasa/humility-in-leadership_b_6038318.html. Accessed October 29, 2015.

[88] Jim Collins. Good to Great. (New York: Harper Collins Publishers), 2001, p. 30.

When humility is considered as a virtue, humility may be seen as an agent of transformation.

As discussed in *Character and Virtue-The Foundation of Authentic Leadership*, influence is defined as:*"the capacity or power of persons or things to be a compelling force that produce effects on the actions, and behavior of others."*

Within this definition, of particular note is the phrase *"compelling force."* The word compelling means, *"having a powerful and irresistible effect."* While the word force suggests *"strength or power exerted upon an object or power and the ability to convince."*[89] In other words, what this simply means is that because they are in positions of influence, aligned with humility as transformational leaders, their aim is to exert and compel others to success as well as the organizations success. Their personal influence becomes an irresistible, compelling force of change for the organization where members of the team desire to follow and emulate their leadership due to the process of transformation. Creating influence that transforms for some may appear to be a daunting leadership task. Consider the following as a place to begin increasing your leadership influence:

- Cultivate Reliability through Consistency
- Be Assertive, Not Aggressive
- Be Flexible Without Compromising
- Maintaining Your Focus On Your Purpose

[89] IBID. Accessed January 30, 2015.

- Consideration of Others
- Practice What You Preach

Cultivate Reliability through Consistency

Reliability is that leadership quality that leads others not just to believe you, but to believe *in* you. Someone can believe and accept what you say is true concerning the weather forecast or the current time. It is another matter altogether for a team member or employee to *believe in you* as a leader. Consistency of organizational standards and operations, equal and fair treatment for everyone, no marks of favoritism, a leader that is as consistent as the sun rising in the morning and setting in the evening is what cultivates an uncommon level of dependability that can be counted on to be true. A work environment of this nature will always succeed.

Be Assertive, Not Aggressive

The Concise Oxford Dictionary defines assertiveness as: *"Forthright, positive, insistence on the recognition of one's rights."* In other words, assertiveness means standing up for your personal rights - expressing thoughts, feelings and beliefs in direct, honest and appropriate ways.

Aggressive behavior fails to consider the views or feelings of other individuals. Those behaving aggressively are intent on getting their point across regardless to any collateral damage they may cause to the team or organization.

To be spoken to aggressively, the receiver can be left wondering what instigated such behavior or what he or she has done to deserve the aggression further impacting the solidarity of the team and the organization. Aggression can prove itself to be a cancer that causes *regression* rather than *progression* in relationships and it cannot be allowed to infect the rest of the team. Interpersonal communication training will assist with this process for these types of behaviors.

Be Flexible Without Compromising

An old adage simply says, *"blessed are the flexible for they shall not be bent out of shape."* A tree that is solidly planted in the ground when the wind comes may bend or sway, but because of the strength of its roots it will always come back to its original state. The winds of change are always blowing, but a leader that is uncompromising in his or her values and standards, will not be bent out of shape. In this type of leadership posture, team members or employee's gain a greater respect for the integrity of a leader of this nature and will also aspire to operate in this manner.

Maintaining Your Focus On Your Purpose

Maintaining your focus on your purpose. It is your purpose that will always answer the question why we are here and a part of this organization.

Here is the scenario. We are all members of a paper company and we all live in New York City and we're trying to get to Orlando, Florida for the annual company conference. Some may want to fly; some may catch a train or some may want to drive. The purpose is for us to get to Orlando for the annual company conference. *How* we get there is not as important as to *why* we are going there. If our why is strong enough, nothing will keep us from getting to Orlando. *Why* we are going is to learn the latest and greatest techniques for making paper. There is an anticipation that *when* we get there the purpose or *why* of our trip will be fulfilled. If our purpose is to be the best paper company, we cannot be distracted by thoughts or investigating how to make plastic cups! Creating influence that transforms means that the leader must maintain the operations in alignment with the purpose of the organization. When our car is out of alignment, it must be realigned or it will eventually cause the tires to wear out prematurely, this costs money. Periodic realignment as to why we are a part of the company to which we belong provides fresh insight and renewed ability to maintain our focus on our purpose that benefits the entire organization and will save everybody money!

Consideration of Others

Consideration of others is an uncommon level of respect that is unsurpassed by outward or external circumstances or situations, good and bad. When team members or employees experience their leaders *"C.A.R.E."* influence increases because they know that they belong to an organization that cares.

Concern in the sense of that which affects or applies to me personally as a member of the organization. When people know that as a leader you are genuinely concerned about their well-being and success, it creates a greater degree of authenticity in the leader to the led relationship. *Altruism* is that leader attribute that puts others before self. The altruistic leader is devoted to the welfare and success of others. When someone is *refreshed* it carries the meaning of renewed strength and vigor. Members of your team or employee's may not always remember everything that you said, but they will never forget how you made them feel and this provides strength and renewal. To *encourage* is to add courage. When fear, failure or discouraging circumstances arise for a team member, the leader that *C.A.R.E.*'s has the opportunity to fill the void or absence of courage. Ambrose Redmon said, *"courage is not the absence of fear, but rather the judgment that something else is more important."* The leader that *C.A.R.E.*'s helps team members and the organization identify what that something is.

Practice What You Preach

Concerning practice, someone once said, *"Don't practice until you get it right. Practice until you can't get it wrong."* Practicing your leadership influence is not about perfection. It is about efficiency and effectiveness. In whatever situation where you'd like to achieve a certain outcome, think through the influencing style that you believe will work best in that situation, and give it a try. As you go, you will grow. Determine what works and what doesn't. As you build your capability and confidence through practice you will become more proficient and see your leadership influence increase.

Whether you are leading, following, and/or collaborating, chances are you need to influence others to be successful. There are a wide range of influence strategies that the transformational leader can utilize. Strategies such as personal relationships, from reliance on key organizational positions, exchange of benefits to encouragement and collaboration. The key is knowing which approach to use in order to obtain the desired results.[90] With this first component of inspirational influence as the launching pad, creating this persona and image within one's leadership portfolio is paramount and essential.

---

[90] IBID.

Once this platform is established, the other three components of transformational leadership provide fundamental support to the process of both being transformed personally and the aim of transforming others organizationally.

PART II: CREATING MOTIVATION THAT TRANSFORMS

. . . .

"People often say that motivation doesn't last. Neither does bathing - that's why we recommend it daily!"

~Zig Ziglar

When we consider the second component of transformational leadership, *inspirational motivation*, the idea simply is to motivate others. Yet in order to do this, there must be a common goal or purpose that people *want* to move towards. In 1997, shoe giant Nike released its marketing ad "Failure" featuring Michael Jordan. In the ad Jordan stated, *"I have missed more than 9,000 shots in my career. I have lost almost 300 games. On 26 occasions I have been entrusted to take the game winning shot, and I missed. I have failed over and over and over again in my life. And that is why I succeed."*[91] Michael Jordan was drafted by the Chicago Bulls on Tuesday, June 19, 1984 in New York, New York and failure or losing is what motivated him to win.[92] On many occasions during his career, Michael's ability to motivate his teammates inspired his teammates to move towards the common goal of becoming world champions.

---

[91] http://www.businessinsider.com/25-nike-ads-that-shaped-the-brands-history-2013. Accessed January 30, 2015.
[92] http://www.basketball-reference.com/draft/NBA_1984. Accessed January 30, 2015.

NBA.com provides us with a snapshot of Jordan's extraordinary career as a professional basketball player. "Six-time NBA champion (1991-93, 1996-98); NBA MVP (1988, '91, '92, '96, '98); 10-time All-NBA First Team (1987-93, 1996-98); All-NBA Second Team (1985); Defensive Player of the Year (1988); Nine-time All-Defensive First Team (1988-93, 1996-98); Rookie of the Year (1985); 14-time All-Star; All-Star MVP (1988, '96, '98); One of 50 Greatest Players in NBA History (1996); Two-time Olympic gold medalist (1984, '92)."[93]

Vince Lombardi once said, *"Leadership is based on a spiritual quality; the power to inspire, the power to inspire others to follow."* [94] The rewards of athletic competition have always been a catalyst for the hard work and dedication necessary to win. The motivation to win the championship for one's city or school is an extremely powerful incentive. We are often motivated and inspired by our sports athletes, our favorite actor, and sometimes by our elected officials. These are persons that many times are interviewed by the media or are often in the spotlight because of their achievements. However, it is important to note that everyday there are ordinary people that do extraordinary things to inspire and motivate us.

The National Institute of Education, Nanyang Technological University in Singapore conducted a

---

[93] http://www.nba.com/history/players/jordan_bio. Accessed January 30, 2015.

[94] http://www.greatest-inspirational-quotes.com/vince-lombardi-quotes. Accessed January 31, 2015.

study entitled *"What Motivates Teachers?"* Some of the responses from the teachers are certainly inspirational. One teacher stated that, *"I'm motivated because I see the needs of the students. When kids have problems and they come to us and we are able to give them some advice, because many of them don't have people to turn to."*[95]

Another teacher responded, *"When you see students achieving so much, from nothing in the beginning, there is a sense of pride, a sense of gratification...and when they leave, you know that you have done a job well and you know that they will continue to do well...and you have made an impression on them."*[96] A third teacher provides perhaps the most applicable comment to being a transformational leader. *"Many of the children have very little sense of self-value and in their family, parents are so busy making ends meet they have no time for them. In school if we can give them a little more time, talk to them and help them in character building...this is not just a job for me, it's a vocation, a calling."*[97]

These three teachers in Singapore are simply examples of ordinary people that are doing extraordinary things to inspire and motivate their students.

---

[95] Low Guat Tin, Lim Lee Hean and Yeap Lay Leng. What Motivates Teachers? New Horizons in Education No.37-1, National Institute of Education, Nanyang Technological University, 1996, Singapore, p. 3.
[96] IBID, p.4.
[97] IBID, p.6.

Most of us, if not all of us can remember those teachers that inspired us, by believing in us which motivated us towards the common goal or purpose of succeeding as responsible adults. As children or teenagers we may not have yet clearly understood what we wanted to do or where we were going in life. However, there were some inspirational and motivational teachers that understood their purpose as educators. Much like this third unknown teacher above in Singapore that stated; *"this is not just a job for me, it's a vocation, a calling.* Considering inspirational motivation from an organizational perspective, Susan M. Heathfield says that, *"the inspirational leader feels passionately about the vision and mission of the organization. He or she is also able to share that passion in a way that enables others to feel passionate, too."*[98]

Heathfield also states that to experience inspiration, people need to feel *included.* Inclusion goes beyond the listening and feedback; for real inclusion, people need to feel intimately connected to the actions and process that are leading to the accomplishment of the goals or the decision of the organization. [99] Important to inspiration is the *integrity* of the person leading. Team members must *trust* and *believe* in their leader to be inspired. Your person or persona is as important as the direction you provide.

---

[98] http://humanresources.about.com/od/leadership/a/ leader_inspire.htm. Accessed January 31, 2015.
[99] IBID.

Employees or team members will always look up to and be inspired by a person who tells the truth, endeavors to do the right things, lives a good life and does their best. A leader's actions play out on the stage of the organization. With this, the team or staff, will boo, cheer and vote with actions that corresponds to what they see and experience from their leaders. [100]

The great film director Alford Hitchcock once stated that, *"When an actor comes to me and wants to discuss his character, I say, 'It's in the script.' If he says, 'But what's my motivation?' I say, 'Your salary.'"*[101] The inspirational leader understands that, while money is a tremendous motivator, so are praise, recognition, rewards, a thank you and noticing an individual's contribution to the success of the organization.

[100] IBID.
[101] http://thinkexist.com/quotes/alfred_hitchcock/. Accessed January 30, 2015.

PART III: CREATING STIMULATION THAT TRANSFORMS

"The ones who are crazy enough to think they can change the world, are the ones that do."

~Anonymous

Intellectual stimulation is the component of transformational leadership that urges *innovation* and *creativity* in team members. Ideas for reframing problems and approaching old situations in new ways are encouraged. Another means of implementing this aspect of transformational leadership is to ask the question of team members, *"How can we do what we do better?"*

This is accomplished without regard to one's status or position in the organization. An authentic transformational leader recognizes that every member of their team is there to contribute to the success and mission accomplishment of their organization.

If this were not so, that particular team member would not have been invited to become an employee. Employing intellectual stimulation within the organization fosters an environment in which *growth, learning,* and *creativity* are valued to the degree that the potential for new standards becomes a constant or norm.

A very basic definition of creativity is simply the *"ability to transcend or rise above traditional ideas, rules in order to create meaningful new ideas, and methods for progressiveness.*"[102] When innovation and creativity is encouraged, the intrinsic rewards or the satisfaction employees feel is an intangible benefit for the company. If team members *feel* like their ideas and creativity are welcomed and considered by the organization, they will do their part and beyond.

According to cognitive psychologist Robert J. Sternberg, creativity can be broadly defined as "*... the process of producing something that is both original and worthwhile.*"[103] Creativity is all about finding new ways of solving problems and approaching situations. Creativity is a skill that can be developed by any and all that understand its necessity. [104] There are many paths to creating or stimulating creativity. Consider the following suggestions:

Commit Yourself to Developing Your Creativity

A commitment is a pledge, promise or obligation that one makes. Someone once said that the journey of 1000 miles begins by taking the first step. The commitment to develop one's creativity is that first step.

---

[102] www.dictionary.com. Accessed February 1, 2015.

[103] http://psychology.about.com/od/cognitivepsychology/tp/ how-to-boost-creativity. Accessed February 1, 2015.

[104] http://psychology.about.com/od/cognitivepsychology/tp/ how-to-boost-creativity. Accessed February 2, 2015.

Build Your Confidence

Confidence means full trust, and belief in one's self and abilities. If you do not believe in yourself, it will be difficult for others to believe in you. *"Trust yourself. Create the kind of self that you will be happy to live with all your life. Make the most of yourself by fanning the tiny, inner sparks of possibility into flames of achievement."* Golda Meir

Overcome Negative Attitudes That Block Creativity

Overcoming negative attitudes is a choice. Choose to take control of your present day circumstances that lead to your future. Choose people that support you, these are the ones that really matter in establishing your creativity. For those that don't support you they don't matter. *"Believe in yourself. Ignore those who try to discourage you. Avoid negative sources, people, places, things and habits. Don`t give up and don`t give in."* Wanda Hope Carter

Fight Your Fear of Failure

Atychiphobia is the fear of failure; fear of not being good enough. It is a fear of confidence in one's own abilities. [105] Someone once said that, everything you've

---

[105] http://www.fearof.net/. Accessed October 26, 2015.

ever wanted is on the other side of fear. Move to the other side of fear which is faith. *"Whenever you find yourself doubting how far you can go, just remember how far you've come. Remember everything you have faced, all the battles you have won, and all the fears that you have overcome."* Unknown

Challenge Yourself

Challenge yourself to improve. The largest room in the world is the room for improvement and always remind yourself that it is not about being perfect. It is about intentionality and determination.

It is the fuel of intentionality and determination that produces transformation one day at a time. Practice, preparation and endless repetition are the ancestors of intentionality and determination. This is how change occurs. Keep going, and remember why you started. You change the world one life at a time and you begin with intention and determination to change yourself for the aim and purpose of helping others to change by challenging self.

Look For Sources of Inspiration

People and situations that inspire us invoke new possibilities by helping us to see and transcend our ordinary experiences and limitations. Our experiences are just that. Our experiences in life are not all that there is to experience. Sources of inspiration carries us from lethargy to possibility.

Create Opportunities For Creativity

The opportunities that we have are not the work of others. They are birthed from within. We create our own opportunities by a *consistent pursuit* of them. Each day is another opportunity for creating. We *create* the opportunity that we need and then *build* the answer to what we have created. Milton Berle once said, *"if opportunity doesn't knock, build a door."*

Kevin Costner in the movie Field of Dreams said, *"If you build it, they will come."* The world has need of your creativity. Don't let the world lack what is on the inside of you. It was A.A. Milne that said, *"Always remember that you are braver than you believe you are, stronger than you appear and smarter than you know."*

Listen to Music

Whatever your favorite style of music is find time daily just to listen to music. Whether its jazz or, country and western, it doesn't matter what style of music it may be. In the musical beats there are harmonies and cords that have come together to create the song that we enjoy. Music has an ability to help us reflect on the message and melodies of the song. Find songs that inspire you and your creativity will increase.

Meditate On What Gives You Peace

To meditate means to give intense thought to, to contemplate, to have in mind or to reflect. It is a means to pause and think purposely and reflectively. This will mean to slow *everything* down, activities, thoughts, etc. Meditation is often, and rightly so, connected to many religious practices. However, it can also simply mean a calming and quieting of one's self. As human beings and as leaders, we were not created to *always* operate in overdrive or 5th gear as many of us consistently do. Peace can be defined as freedom from distractions and annoyances.

It can also be defined as a state or condition conducive to or characterized by tranquility. Such as the peace provided by a secluded mountain or beach resort. Find or discover for the first time or discover again those aspects of life and leadership that give you peace and meditate on those things. Creativity is capable of thriving in times and places like these.

Color Outside The Lines

When we were in kindergarten and the first grade we were always told to color inside the lines. Creativity pushes and challenges you to color outside the lines. Outside of limitations that have been established is a wealth of creativity to be discovered. This is the place where there no boundaries or limits. Go beyond self-imposed limitations and the limitations that others have placed on you. There is more inside of you to be discovered and released. Color outside the boundaries and limitations of ethnicity, gender, or socio-economic status and be transformed by what is on the inside that you have released.

Don't Expect Perfection

Achieving perfection in *anything* is unrealistic when we recognize that we are imperfect. What is achievable is quality and excellence. If we aim for perfection, we will certainly achieve quality and excellence and that which stimulates us to create will inspire others because of its nature.

Do Something That You Have Never Done Before

It has often been said that variety is the spice of life. If we're locked into a routine, and it has been the same routine for 10, 15, or 20 years it is time to take a risk. Taking risks are never comfortable. Oprah Winfrey once stated, *"Do the one thing you think you cannot do. Fail at it. Try again. Do better the second time. The only people who never tumble are those who never mount the high wire. This is your moment."* Challenge yourself to do something that you have never done before and watch the creativity arise.

Learn To Ask More Questions

We may ask questions but are they the right questions to be asked. When we learn to ask more questions, the answers have the potential to carry us mentally to a place or position that we had not thought about simply because we have learned to ask more questions! People ask a lot of questions but sometimes it's not the right question therefore you cannot get the answer you may be looking for because it was the wrong question! Learn to ask more questions for creativity and make sure that it is the right question.

Don't Compare Yourself to Others

Don't compare yourself to anybody else because when you were created there was no one else created with your voice pattern or sound, no one else created with your fingerprints, there was no one else created with your unique makeup.

You are designed that way on purpose because there is no else like you. Leonardo da Vinci painted only *one* Mona Lisa. As you stimulate and stir up your unique contributions to the world in which we live, others will discover what you have discovered about yourself. I am a designer original and there is no one else like me *anywhere* in the world.

Become Comfortable With Silence

It is important that the capable leader learns to become comfortable with silence. Everywhere we go there is noise, which many times equates to distractions which does not allow us to concentrate or focus on our purpose. Learn to get to a quiet place away from the car horns, away from the cell phones, away from the TV, away from the hustle and bustle of the world in which we live.

It has been said by some, *"It's so loud in here that I can't hear myself think!"* It is because the world in which we live is loud. Getting to a place to be alone and in silence, a place of solitude will enable creativity to flow as it intended. Uninterrupted and unhindered. This will not be easy because there is always something or someone that needs you. To be the best *you*, develop the discipline and create the time in your schedule so you can be alone to hear yourself think and stimulate your creativity.

Fall in Love With What You Do

Someone once said that if you find a job that you love you will never have to work a day in your life. When you love what you do, the passion of your purpose is obvious. To keep your passion and purpose alive, invest or mentor someone else. Never allow *anyone* to rain on your parade. This is the profession that I have chosen and I love it! Someone else may not, but the passion for what I do, and the purpose behind why I do it is rewarding. When you love what you do, you are capable of celebrating others promotions and successes. When you love what you do, it will be important to associate with other like-minded people. Always remember that people are like elevators. They will either take you up or they will take you down! Focus on continuing to develop professionally, and decide to color outside the lines, love people (even those that don't like you) and love the journey. Creativity will be stimulated and you will never work a day in your life. It is important to note as we move to the next section that sometimes the greatest source of inspiration is in you. ***Don't ever to forget to simply look in the mirror.***

PART IV: CREATING CONSIDERATION THAT TRANSFORMS

··

"There are two types of people who will tell you that you cannot make a difference in this world: those who are afraid to try and those who are afraid you will succeed."

Ray Goforth

Individualized consideration is that aspect of transformational leadership that focuses on individual members needs for *achievement* and *growth*. This is where the transformational leader acts as coach or mentor. Individualized consideration is practiced when new learning opportunities are created along with a supportive climate. From the viewpoint of this session, consideration is defined as an *uncompromising level of respect that is unhindered by external factors or behaviors*. If a relationship of trust has not been established between the leader and the led the aim of individualized consideration may be very challenging.

For those that have been in the workplace for any length of time, the relationships that have been established or the *lack* of relationships that have been established prove for some to be an internal source of struggle. Everyone wants to fit in and feel like they belong or are accepted organizationally. To possess the mindset of doing one's job is certainly what is expected by the organization.

However, the expectation of job accomplishment does little for cohesiveness and unity amongst departments and team members of the organization. Where there has been distrust and painful memories for members of your organization or team, apprehensions and suspicions of *"more of the same"* may be present. The individualized considerate leader *becomes* a skilled listener and communicator to identify any potential relationship barriers both personally and corporately.

Chinese poet and philosopher Lao Tsu says, *"If you want to know me, look inside your heart."* If authentic transformation is to occur individually it must be from *"heart to heart."* If what Lao Tsu suggests is correct and if consideration is indeed an uncompromising level of respect that is unhindered by external factors or behaviors, what is the nature or substance of these two principles? Although this is certainly not an exhaustive list, there are three components offered in this section for reflection:

- Focus on Employee or Team Member
- Discover Their Dreams and Aspirations
- Demonstrate Your Intent To Help Them Grow

Focus on Employee or Team Member

The first objective in these discussions is to address any questions or concerns the team member may have. It is a time of purposeful dialogue and not a monologue. Secondly, identify what's happening in your employees' life that both supports and challenges them and their work performance. Seek to discover what motivates them and those things that are most important to them. Simple questions such as, *"how are you doing?"* and *"how is your family?"* creates a natural bridge for meaningful dialogue. Thirdly, as an individualized considerate leader you want to discover their short and long-term career aspirations and to assist in creating a developmental plan to achieve these aspirations.

In the final moments of the discussion, ask for suggestions on how the organization or you as their leader can improve. Opening up to employees or team members in this manner creates incalculable value in your trust account with those that follow you.

Discover Their Dreams and Aspirations

An aspiration is a strong desire to achieve something. A dream is defined here as a deep imagined, aspiration or hope. Merriam Webster's dictionary says that to discover means *"to see, find or be made aware of something for the first time."* A simple straight forward question from the individualized considerate leader asks, *"What are the things I can do to help you achieve your dreams and aspirations?"* If as an individualized considerate leader you have connected with your employees or team members, this is the opportunity to allow them to express their dreams and aspirations to you as a leader.

It is uncommon for people to be able to come into the workplace and express with their boss, their aspirations and dreams. As an employee or team member has the opportunity to express their dreams and aspirations it creates an uncommon feeling of safety and security. Which in essence, creates an uncommon loyalty to the organization. All because as an individualized considerate leader, an *uncompromising level of respect, unhindered by external factors or behaviors* was honestly experienced by a team member.

This idea lends further support to Lao Tsu's principle of *if you want to know me, look inside your heart* or the concept of from *heart to heart*. The individualized considerate leader has a heart to understand that everyone has dreams and aspirations and will do everything possible to help team members in achieving them.

Demonstrate Your Intent To Help Them Grow

This is where the individualized considerate leader assists in helping the team member to qualify or prepare for greater responsibility within the organization that leads to the potential for promotion. As a leader, there are times when a person will believe that they are ready for a promotion or higher level assignment. If a team member or employee is *not ready* for the promotion, *they are not ready*. Team members or employees may see others get promoted ahead of them which can become a significant emotional event within the organization. However, if as a leader you assist the team member to develop the skills lacking and a plan to acquire the necessary skills for the promotion, this will help to assure the team member of the power of partnership; we are in this together and we are better together. A partner does his or her part. The leader's part is to observe, develop and train each team member. The team member's or employee's part is to make the effort to learn and acquire the lessons of the training that is beneficial both personally and organizationally.

If a viable, honest development plan is in place, tailored to the team member or employee and functioning this will assist the employee or team member to see for themselves the need for consistent growth and preparation for the future. A plan of this nature may include:

- Regularly scheduled mentoring sessions and development planning for the future.
- Within the development plan of growth, assist the team member to set measurable and achievable goals for continued development.
- Regularly scheduled mentoring sessions (bi-monthly or quarterly) to revise and monitor progress, make revisions to the plan as needed, and acknowledge results.

The individualized considerate leader makes it clear that these sessions are not about *criticism,* it is an honest *critic* rooted in observation over a period of time. Criticism without correction and instruction leaves nothing but a wake of negativity. The more popular understanding of a critic is that of a person who tends to make harsh, captious, judgements or simply one who finds fault. However, on the positive side a critic may also be known as a person who judges, evaluates, or analyzes.

When team members or employees know honest, unbiased evaluation of their work performance is a part of their growth and increase potential of promotion the following proverb comes alive: *"people don't care how much you know, until they know how much you care."* [106] To carry this proverb further, we may rightly conclude that people don't care how much you know until they know how much you *care about them personally!*

Individualized consideration is the aspect of transformational leadership that encourages an uncompromising level of respect that is unhindered by external factors or behaviors for every employee or team member. It is this level of respect for every member of the team that will gain support and loyalty for the organization that will transform all that desire to be transformed.

---

[106] http://www.goodreads.com/quotes/34690-people-don-t-care-how-much-you-know-until-they-know.

Every organization is made of a team of employee's with varying degrees of abilities and potential. The individualized considerate leader takes into account the fact that no one is like any other one on the team and the goal for everyone is transformation to the next juncture of leadership. *"True leaders don't create more followers, they create more leaders."* Tom Peters

Summation: Creating Transformational Leaders Who Transform Others
....

Transformational leadership emerged as a concept began with the book by the political scientist James MacGregor Burns titled *"Leadership"* in 1978. According to Burns, transformational leadership is seen and experienced when *"leaders and followers make each other to advance to a higher level of morality and motivation."* Through the strength of their vision and personality, transformational leaders are able to inspire followers to change expectations, perceptions, and motivations to work towards common goals.

It is grounded in positive change of the emotions, values, ethics, standards for the accomplishment of long-term goals of individuals and organizations. Transformational leadership is also concerned with follower's motives, satisfying their needs and incorporating their ideals into the process of transformation. It is a leadership style that can inspire positive changes in those who follow. Transformational leaders are generally energetic, enthusiastic, and passionate. This type of leader is concerned, focused and engaged in helping every member of the team to succeed via the process of transformational leadership.

Phillip V. Lewis stated that the goal of a transformational leader is to *"transform people and organizations: change minds and hearts; enlarge vision, insight, and understanding; clarify purposes; make behavior congruent with beliefs, principles, and values; and bring about changes that are permanent, self-perpetuating, and momentum building."*

According to Bernard Bass, transformational leaders *"earn trust, respect, and admiration from their followers"* and in essence this is what produces the transformation. Bass suggests that there are four components of transformational leadership:

1. Idealized Influence
2. Inspirational Motivation
3. Intellectual Stimulation
4. Individualized Consideration

To transform is to change in appearance or structure. It further means to change the condition, nature or character of something. Of the many diverse types and styles of leadership, transformational leadership aims for a metamorphosis of character. Transformational leaders understand the necessity of consistent and perpetual transformation. By creating transformational leaders that transform others, the character transformation of the organization is set in motion and it is this motion that creates momentum for perpetual success.

QUESTIONS FOR REFLECTION

. . . .

1. What practical steps could you make to adapt the four components of transformational leadership into your present style of leadership in your organization?

2. What is the main idea of transformational leadership and how would you persuade your team members or employees to intentionally develop this style of leadership?

3. Mohandas Gandhi as a transformational leader *stated that, "You must be the change you wish to see in the world."* Which of the 4 I's of transformational leadership requires the most development for you personally as a leader if you are to become the change that you wish to see in the world?

4. You have been selected to explain why transformational leadership either works or will not work in your organization. Taking either position, what principles from this session prove your point?

5. Which component of transformational leadership if implemented today do you believe would have the most impact on your organization? Qualify your answer.

QUOTES OF PRINCIPLED LEADERS

"I can affect change by transforming the only thing that I ever had control over in the first place and that is myself."

Deepak Chopra

"The secret of change is to focus not on fighting the old, but on building the new."

Socrates

"You are far too smart to be the only thing standing in your way."

Jennifer Freeman

"The first step toward success is taken when you refuse to be a captive of the environment in which you find yourself."

Mark Caine

"You can make excuses all you want. But at the end of the day all you'll have are poor excuses and another wasted day."

Unknown

Notes: _____

_____

_____

_____

_____

_____

_____

_____

_____

_____

_____

_____

_____

_____

_____

_____

_____

_____

_____

_____

_____

_____

_____

_____

_____

_____

_____

_____

Notes: _____

_____

_____

_____

_____

_____

_____

_____

_____

_____

_____

_____

_____

_____

_____

_____

_____

_____

_____

_____

_____

_____

_____

_____

_____

_____

_____

_____

_____

_____

_____

_____

_____